THE USBORNE BOOK OF TH
PARANORMA

Anna Claybourne, Gillian Doherty,
Gill Harvey, Philippa Wingate

Designed by Stephen Wright
and Michèle Busby

Studio photography by Howard Allman
Illustrated by Gary Bines, Jeremy Gower
and Darrell Warner

Edited by Philippa Wingate

Consultants: John and Anne Spencer;
Caroline Watt, Department of Psychology,
University of Edinburgh

Digital images and textures created by John Russell

Picture research by Ruth King

CONTENTS

WHAT IS THE PARANORMAL?

The word "paranormal" simply means "beyond normal". It suggests that there are two categories of events - some that are normal, and some that are not. This categorization is based on our belief that things can't be normal if science doesn't have an explanation for them.

Paranormal activities

"The paranormal" is a general term for all paranormal subjects or happenings. These range from spoon bending to UFO sightings and spooky hauntings. This book covers the four most well-documented areas – poltergeists, extra-sensory perception, ghosts, and aliens.

 ### Poltergeists and ghosts

Poltergeists show themselves by what they do, for example making noises or moving things around. They are often thought of as a type of ghost, but they are usually invisible. Ghosts are generally visions or apparitions – in other words, people can see them. Victims of either poltergeists or ghosts are referred to as "haunted".

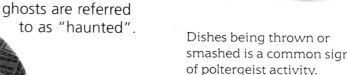

Dishes being thrown or smashed is a common sign of poltergeist activity.

The sighting of these strange craft gave rise to the term "flying saucers" in 1947.

Extra-sensory perception

Extra-sensory perception is often shortened to ESP. "Extra" is another way of saying beyond, so ESP means experiences we couldn't have had via our sight, smell, hearing, taste or touch. Most scientists believe we learn all we know through our senses, but if ESP exists, we may learn things in other, more mysterious ways.

It's possible that ESP is caused by "brain waves" between minds.

Aliens

Most people think of aliens as beings from outer space who visit our planet in Unidentified Flying Objects, or UFOs.

If you see a UFO, it's called a close encounter of the first kind. If a UFO leaves a mark, like a burn on the ground, it is an encounter of the second kind. In an encounter of the third kind, you actually meet aliens. The fourth kind is alien abduction. This book covers all four kinds of encounter.

Case studies

There are twenty case studies in this book that give exciting accounts of paranormal events, based on the claims of the people involved. The paranormal is hard to predict or record, however, so it is difficult to be sure they really happened. Even if people were telling the truth in their accounts, their imagination or memory may have played tricks on them; and some accounts may be hoaxes. So how can you find out the truth?

The evidence

All you can do is look closely at the evidence, then decide for yourself whether you believe the stories or not. To help you, there is an assessment after each case study. This examines the details of the story, and factors that may have affected it.

CHAPTER ONE: POLTERGEISTS?

WHAT ARE POLTERGEISTS?

Poltergeists are mysterious presences, forces or ghosts. They usually haunt their victims by moving things or throwing them through the air. Other common forms of poltergeist activity are smashing dishes, or making rapping noises. This is how poltergeists got their name, which is German for "noisy ghost".

Other strange events, such as changes in temperature, unexplained fires or the appearance of objects out of nowhere, are also attributed to poltergeists. Sometimes, people have claimed to see them, too.

Do they really exist?

Poltergeist cases have been reported for nearly 2,000 years, ever since the historian Titus Livius described stones being mysteriously hurled at Roman soldiers. In recent times, dozens of poltergeists have been reported all over the world – yet very few pieces of concrete evidence have been produced to prove that they do exist.

Are they harmful?

Whatever causes poltergeist activity, it usually seems to be mischievous rather than genuinely harmful. Many poltergeists seem to enjoy making fun of people, especially paranormal investigators.

There are exceptions to this, however, and some accounts describe scary attempts to inflict injury on people. Thankfully, this is very rare.

If you ever encounter a poltergeist, it might do its best to frighten you. However, the chances are that you will remain completely unharmed.

This 16th-century woodcut, showing a demon pushing a man, is thought to be an attempt to illustrate a poltergeist haunting.

Case study 1: EERIE ENFIELD

Date: August 31st, 1977
Place: Enfield, London, UK
Witnesses: Multiple witnesses

THE EVENTS

Janet Harper lay trembling in bed – but not with fear. It was the bed itself that was shaking. And she could hear strange shuffling noises, like footsteps. Janet and her brother Pete shouted for their mother, but then the shaking stopped.

The shaking returns

The next night, the family realized that there was definitely something spooky going on. The shaking returned, along with loud bangs. Then a heavy chest of drawers suddenly shuffled across the floor, all by itself. Terrified, the Harpers fled next door and called the police.

The chair slowly rotated as it shuffled across the floor.

More mysteries

The policewoman who arrived, Officer Heeps, couldn't believe her eyes. A kitchen chair crept across the floor, as if pushed by an unseen hand.

The police were baffled, and couldn't find any explanation. Eventually, the Harpers had no choice but to move back into their home.

However, over the next few weeks, more strange events occurred. Toys flew through the air, and were mysteriously hot to the touch. There were sudden cold breezes, and furniture lurched around, terrorizing the family.

Marbles and toy bricks flew through the air, bombarding members of the family.

As the haunting continued, journalists and investigators from the Society for Psychical Research[1] came to the house. One scientist was hit on the head by a toy brick.

Janet was usually nearby when odd things occurred. Could she somehow have something to do with the poltergeist that was haunting her home?

[1]See page 48

Up in the air

After a while, Janet and her sister Rose began to be dragged out of bed by a strange force. Janet often fell asleep in her own bed, but woke up somewhere else.

David Robertson, a scientist, came to investigate whether Janet was really levitating, which means defying gravity by floating through the air. Janet went into her bedroom, and soon called out that she was flying. But when Robertson tried to go in, he couldn't open the door. It was completely stuck.

However, a milkman and an old woman, who had both been outside in the street at the time, reported something very odd. They said they had seen Janet through the window, floating and moving up and down in the air among a whirling mass of books and toys. The milkman, who had previously refused to believe gossip about the poltergeist, was petrified.

Later, a photographer called Graham Morris did manage to take some photographs of Janet in bizarre positions.

One photograph appeared to show Janet floating through the air.

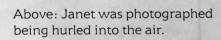

Above: Janet was photographed being hurled into the air.

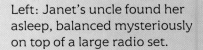

Left: Janet's uncle found her asleep, balanced mysteriously on top of a large radio set.

Case study 1: EERIE ENFIELD

Finding out more

A researcher named Maurice Grosse spent hours making notes of all the odd things he saw at the Harpers' house. These included small fires breaking out, and puddles appearing from nowhere.

The ghost speaks

Grosse tried talking to the poltergeist using rapping noises. The ghost was asked to make one rap for "no" and two for "yes", but its answers were confused.

Then written messages started to appear. The first message read: "I will stay in this house."

Soon after that, the poltergeist started to make barking and whistling noises.

These developed into a deep, gruff man's voice, and Maurice Grosse conducted several conversations with it. The voice seemed to be coming from Janet's throat, but Janet claimed she had no control over it. It was much deeper and rougher than her normal voice. It was also rude, using lots of swear words.

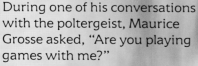

Was a poltergeist throwing toys around the house at Enfield?

During one of his conversations with the poltergeist, Maurice Grosse asked, "Are you playing games with me?"

As if in response to Grosse's question, a toybox flew through the air and hit him on the head.

Voice from the grave?

Grosse became convinced that Janet could not possibly be faking the conversations. He decided to question the voice about its identity. When it responded, it claimed to be the spirit of an old man who had died in the house years earlier. He told them he had died in a chair in the front room, and said that he threw Janet out of bed because it had been his bed when he was alive.

Disturbances caught on camera

There were many attempts to photograph the events at Enfield, but the poltergeist seemed camera-shy. Maurice Grosse even suspected that it had some knowledge of how technical equipment worked.

Photographer Graham Morris found that his equipment repeatedly went wrong, and an expensive camera broke when Maurice Grosse took it into the house. The manufacturers of the camera were baffled by its breakdown, and claimed that the fault was extremely rare. A television reporter's tape recorder also mysteriously became jammed.

The photos that Graham Morris did manage to take, however, are still very hard to explain – unless there really was a poltergeist at work.

These two pictures, taken at one-second intervals, show a pillow that seems to be jumping and twisting by itself.

Teleportation

Teleportation is the name for something disappearing from one place and reappearing in another, often seeming to move through walls or other solid objects. One striking example of teleportation occurred at Enfield.

Mrs. Nottingham, who lived next door, found a book in her house. The book belonged to Janet, but it was on the other side of the wall from Janet's bedroom. No one had carried it there.

There have been other reports of teleportation. This case is of a boy who was haunted by a poltergeist.

One day, the boy was astonished to see his shirt fade away and vanish from his body.

The shirt that had disappeared was later found hanging on a door in his house.

Case study 1: THE ASSESSMENT

The Enfield poltergeist finally died away in 1978, more than a year after it appeared. It looks as if something paranormal, or supernatural, did happen. However, there is very little completely convincing evidence to prove beyond doubt that the Enfield house was haunted.

 ## Was Enfield a hoax?

If so many strange things were really happening, why did it seem so hard to catch them on film?

Some investigators claim that the poltergeist didn't like to be recorded.

Perhaps it avoided photographers and broke equipment deliberately, to avoid being filmed.

Others think this is just an excuse invented by the family to cover up their elaborate hoax.

 ## Expert opinions

The investigators in the Enfield case had various disagreements. Maurice Grosse was sure he had experienced over 1,500 inexplicable events in the house. His colleague, Guy Lyon Playfair, also believed in the poltergeist and wrote a book about it. However, another investigator, Anita Gregory,

Maurice Grosse reading *This House is Haunted*, written by Guy Lyon Playfair

said she never saw anything paranormal in the house. She said the children had told her to cover her face, while they giggled and faked the poltergeist-like events.

Recording equipment, including cameras and tape recorders, mysteriously stopped working in the Enfield house.

Focus on Janet

Janet was definitely the focus for the poltergeist (see page 14). Strange things almost always happened near her, or to her.

Some photographs show Janet's brothers and sisters looking upset, while she laughs or smiles. This might suggest she was playing tricks. But it is common in poltergeist cases for the focus to be unusually calm.

Years later Janet admitted she had sometimes tricked the investigators for fun. But she said most of the poltergeist's activities were real.

Was she faking it?

Janet was photographed floating out of bed, but she could easily have jumped into the positions recorded in the photographs.

A speech therapist who studied the gruff voice said that Janet could have made it herself. If she had half-shut her epiglottis, which blocks your windpipe when you swallow, her voice would have sounded much deeper and rougher.

Other people in the street might have told Janet about the man who had lived in the house. Janet may have decided he seemed a fitting ghost.

Epiglottis

Windpipe

Still unexplained

So many odd events were seen by so many witnesses that it's hard to believe they were all faked.

To this day, the case remains a mystery.

In this photograph, Janet (in the middle) is almost smiling, while Peter and Rose look less happy.

THE FOCUS

Unlike ghosts, poltergeists usually seem to be linked to a particular living person. This person is known as the focus. In most cases, when objects fly around, doors slam or people hear strange noises, the focus is almost always nearby.

Sometimes weird things happen to the focuses themselves as well. They might find themselves being dragged out of bed or up a flight of stairs, or being grabbed by invisible hands. They might go into a trance, and some have even claimed to levitate (float up into the air).

Despite these alarming events, the focus is rarely harmed, and the poltergeist usually disappears after a while.

Typical focuses

Focuses are usually young people aged between 11 and 16, and are often girls rather than boys.

Eleonore Zugun was the focus of an unusual poltergeist in the 1920s in Romania. Strange scratches appeared down her face.

A focus is often someone who is feeling upset or stressed. This might be caused by moving to a new house, by the focus's parents getting divorced, or just by the everyday pressures of being a teenager.

Adults can also be focuses. One poltergeist in France picked on a young mother. Another haunted a 50-year-old man who worked at a gardening shop in Bromley, England. The shop became the scene of dozens of bizarre and scary events.

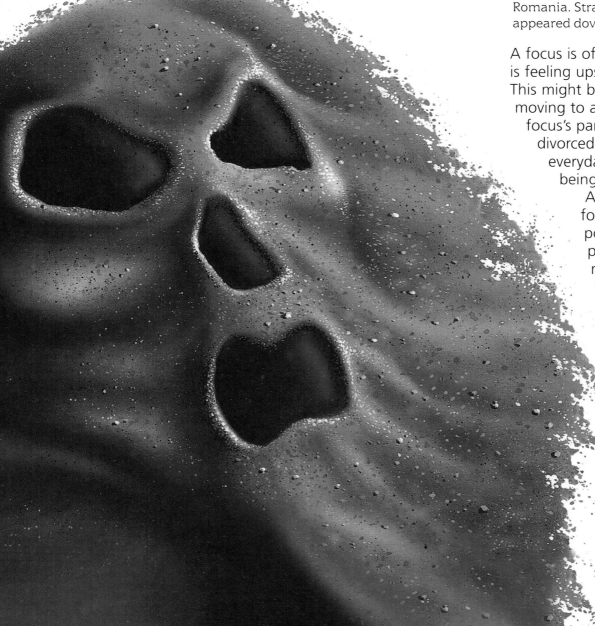

The Bromley poltergeist formed this strange face in a mound of spilled fertilizer.

Can a focus cause a poltergeist?

Some experts think that focuses might even cause the strange occurrences that become known as poltergeist hauntings. It may be that some kind of mental energy, coming from the mind of the focus, is transformed into a physical force that can move objects and make noises. Nobody really knows how this could happen. Most focuses don't want to be bothered by a poltergeist, and they certainly don't seem to cause hauntings deliberately. So these strange mental powers, if they exist, must be subconscious. This means that the person who has them does not know about them, and can't control them.

Some investigators think that stress and worry, especially in teenagers, might somehow be expressed as a physical force.

This physical force could be what causes objects to move by themselves or produces mysterious noises.

Case study 2: HAUNTED HYDESVILLE

Date: March 31st, 1848
Place: Hydesville,
New York, USA
Witnesses: Multiple
witnesses

THE EVENTS

Mr. Michael Weekman never did find out what was causing the odd rumbling and shaking at his house in the village of Hydesville. Instead, he moved out. Mr. and Mrs. Fox and their two youngest children moved in.

They had been there only a few months when they began to hear the peculiar noises – thumping, banging and knocking. Night after night, the trouble continued.

At last the girls, Catherine, 12, and Margaretta, 14, were so unnerved that they started to sleep in the bed in their parents' bedroom.

Surprise replies

One Friday evening the family was in the bedroom and the strange noises were going on as usual. According to Mrs. Fox, Catherine suddenly shouted, "Mr. Splitfoot, do as I do!" Mr. Splitfoot was her name for the devil, and she was challenging the noise to copy her. She clapped her hands several times.

They waited. Then a rapping noise answered with exactly the same number of raps.

Now it was Margaretta's turn. She ordered the spirit, "Now, do as I do. Count one, two, three, four."

Back came the answer: rap, rap, rap, rap.

Margaretta and Catherine Fox, the sisters at the heart of the Hydesville haunting

Who are you?

Then Mrs. Fox decided to test the ghostly being. She asked it to rap out the ages of her seven children in order. It did so, getting all their ages exactly right.

Finally, it made three raps. These were for the youngest child of all, who had died at the age of three. Mrs. Fox shuddered. She was sure a dead spirit was present.

The family devised a code to ask the ghost questions. Spelling out answers, it told them it was the spirit of a salesman named Charles, who had been murdered in the house by having his throat cut. He said he was buried under the cellar floorboards.

The Foxes' haunted house in Hydesville with the sign above the door.

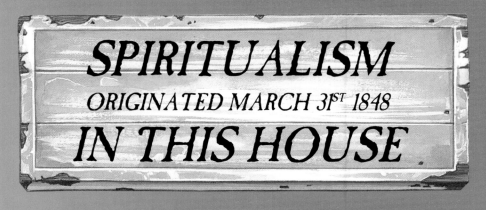

SPIRITUALISM
ORIGINATED MARCH 31ST 1848
IN THIS HOUSE

The Foxes' house now bears this sign.

The news spreads

News of the ghost spread through the village, and hundreds of people flocked to witness the messages for themselves. The newspapers soon picked up the story, and the Foxes became celebrities.

The noises became linked to the two girls. When they moved to the town of Rochester, the rapping went too. The house at Hydesville was then haunted by gruesome gurgling noises. They sounded just like a man dying – from a slit throat.

Fame and fortune

Then the spirit told Catherine and Margaretta to hire a large hall and demonstrate the spooky messages to the public. The show was a great success, and the sisters went on tour. They amassed thousands of loyal followers. Many who witnessed their communication with the spirit believed that, at last, proof existed: there was life after death.

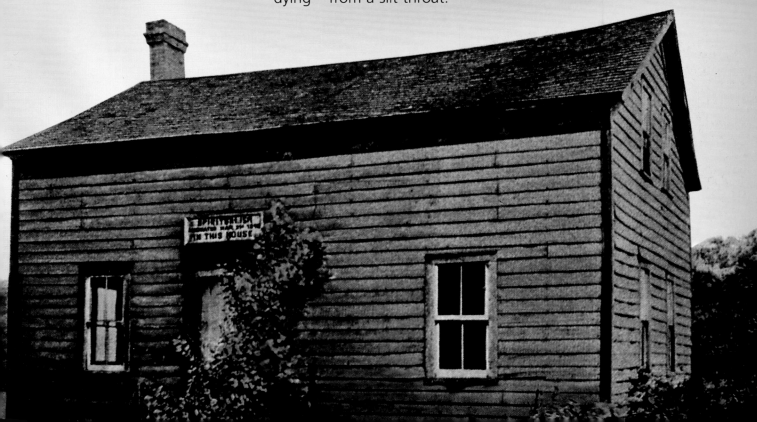

Case study 2: HAUNTED HYDESVILLE

Medium madness

Following the Fox sisters' success, talking to spirits became the height of fashion. The craze became known as Spiritualism (see page 48). Suddenly there were hundreds of mediums – people who claimed they could contact the dead.

In this photograph, a ghost made of the mysterious substance called ectoplasm seems to materialize from a medium's ear.

Mediums held "seances" – meetings where spirits were supposed to communicate with the living. Some mediums even said they could make ghosts appear, formed out of a strange white substance called ectoplasm. But ectoplasm was often faked using fine cloth or paper.

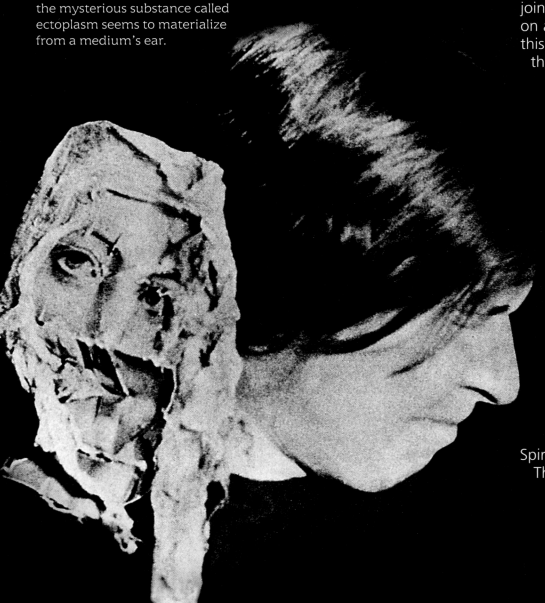

"It's a fraud!"

In 1888, 40 years later, Margaretta called a public meeting. Crowds flocked to hear her, but they were astonished when she shouted, "It's a fraud! Spiritualism is a fraud from beginning to end!"

Margaretta said that she and her sister had faked the rapping noises by cracking joints in their toes. She stood on a table and demonstrated this with several loud knocks that echoed around the hall.

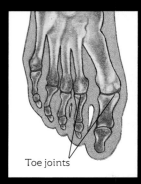

Toe joints

The sisters may have made rapping sounds by cracking their toe joints (shown in red).

A final twist

Surprisingly, many people would not believe Margaretta's confession, and Spiritualism continued as before. Then, three years later, Margaretta retracted her statement. She said the Catholic Church, which she had joined, had forced her to make a false confession rejecting Spiritualism.

Case study 2: THE ASSESSMENT

Because of the huge media attention that surrounded the Fox sisters, it is very hard to tell what really went on in this case. Was Hydesville a hoax?

 ## Could it be true?

It *is* possible that the sisters sometimes faked the noises with their toes. But that doesn't explain the shaking and banging in the Hydesville house at the start of the case, or the very loud knocking that hundreds of villagers witnessed.

 ## Bones in the cellar

Could there have been any truth behind the spirit's story that a murdered salesman was buried in the cellar? This might be possible.

In 1904, some schoolchildren visiting the site of the Hydesville house found a skeleton under a wall that had collapsed. Nearby was a tin box of the type that salesmen carried long ago.

A skull and bones were found at Hydesville. Could they have belonged to a salesman?

Tried and tested

Early in their careers, the Fox sisters were subjected to rigorous tests by scientists. Most of these investigators ended up believing the sisters' claims.

Investigators said they had seen the Fox sisters make tables fly into the air.

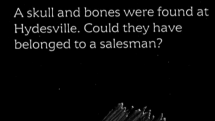 ## A cunning combination?

Perhaps the case of the Fox sisters could be explained by a combination of trickery and real paranormal phenomena.

As the trend for Spiritualism took off, the sisters were under huge pressure to perform on the stage and in front of reporters. Because of this, they may have started to fake some of the rapping sounds.

But the early events, the shuffling, knocking and banging noises focusing on two girls, bear all the hallmarks of an unexplained poltergeist.

Case study 3: MOUNT RAINIER

Date: 1949
Place: Mount Rainier,
Washington State, USA
Witnesses: The
Mannheims

THE EVENTS

Robert Mannheim was fascinated by ghosts. His Aunt Harriet had taught him how to use a Ouija board[1], and 13-year-old Robert hoped that a dead spirit would use the board to send him a message from beyond the grave.

Holy shakes

One evening Robert's parents went out, leaving him at home with his grandmother. That was when a slow, scary dripping sound started echoing from one of the bedrooms. Robert and his grandmother ran to the room, and were shocked to see a painting of Jesus on the wall shaking violently – as if moved by an invisible hand. The room was also haunted by strange scratching noises.

A painting of
Jesus shook
eerily to and fro.

It seemed as if a
ghostly hand was
moving the picture.

[1]See page 22

A death in the family

Just 11 days later, Aunt Harriet died, and Robert used his Ouija board to try to contact her spirit. On one occasion, the family heard footsteps in the haunted bedroom. Robert's mother called out, "Is that you, Harriet?"

She asked the spirit to make three knocks if it was Harriet. At once, three raps echoed around the room.

From then on, Robert became the victim of a poltergeist. Heavy objects were hurled around the house, and Robert was often dragged violently out of his chair onto the floor.

The horrible scratches appearing on Robert's skin often spelled out words or his name.

Robert claimed that his arm was very painful.

Scratched messages

The family tried sending Robert to stay with their priest, Reverend Schulze. But at Schulze's house, he was thrown out of a chair and under a bed. He soon came home again.

Until then, the poltergeist had not been harmful. Now, something truly horrifying happened. Hideous scratches appeared on Robert's skin. They seemed to come, not from the outside of his body, but from the inside.

Possession?

Next, the ghostly presence spoke. A gravelly voice came from Robert's throat. Besides being much deeper than his own speech, sometimes the strange voice spoke in Latin – a language he didn't even know.

The Mannheims were terrified. Speaking in Latin is believed by the Catholic Church to be a sign of "possession"– when a demon takes over a person's body.

A Catholic cure

The Mannheims asked a priest to hold an "exorcism", a religious rite designed to banish evil spirits. The haunting ended, and after his ordeal Robert became a Catholic.

Equipment often used in exorcisms

But can we be sure that Robert was possessed? Could he have been pretending? Or was he the victim of a very clever poltergeist?

In this engraving of an exorcism, demons are shown leaving the victim's body enveloped in a puff of smoke.

Case study 3: THE ASSESSMENT

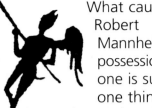

What caused Robert Mannheim's possession? No one is sure. But one thing is certain – Robert had a very active imagination. He was fascinated by ghosts, and he could have faked the scary voice for his own amusement. But the shaking picture, rapping and scratching are still a mystery. They would be much harder to fake.

Imitation?

Poltergeists seem to respond to what is happening around them. Perhaps Robert's poltergeist began to imitate a demon when possession was mentioned. Poltergeists often appear in cases of possession, so the two may be linked.

Exorcism – a cure?

Although exorcism appeared to help Robert, that does not necessarily have to mean that he was really possessed by the devil or a demon.

Instead, it may be that the prayers and rituals of the exorcism ceremony reassured him and helped to calm him down. This may have given him the strength to realize that he had control over his strange situation, allowing him to face the problem and overcome it by himself.

These old engravings show evil demons trying to attack people's souls with spears and arrows.

Ouija boards

Ouija (pronounced "weeja") boards, like the one Robert used, were invented during the 19th-century craze for talking to spirits.

Some people believed dead spirits could spell out messages by moving a pointer or an upturned glass around the letters of the alphabet, which were either painted on a board or printed on a set of cards.

However, to use a Ouija board, people had to put their hands on the pointer as it moved, so it was very easy for someone to cheat.

Letters   Pointer   Board

Spirits were thought to send messages by moving the pointer to different letters on a Ouija board.

WHAT CAUSES POLTERGEISTS?

Poltergeists are among the best-known paranormal phenomena. Yet, despite being so common, they are still very difficult to explain. There are many different theories about what might cause them. Some people think they may be a kind of natural force, and that science will one day explain them. Others think that they are caused by the power of the human mind itself.

Medieval devils

In medieval times, people thought poltergeists were caused by devils or demons. It was believed that devils could possess people by entering and living inside them, making them behave strangely and speak in scary voices.

This demon appears in a book printed in 1631. It seems to be beckoning someone.

Returned from the dead?

One theory suggests poltergeists are ghosts or spirits of the dead, trying to contact the living. Some poltergeists do identify themselves as dead spirits through messages or voices. However, unlike ghosts, poltergeists usually focus on someone who is stressed, and fade away when the person becomes happier. This supports the theory that poltergeists are caused by living humans.

Ghosts, like this one seen at Newby, England, are often thought to be dead people's spirits. It seems likely, however, that poltergeists are caused by something else, although no one is quite sure what.

Case study 4: PONTEFRACT PANIC

Date: August, 1966
Place: Pontefract,
England, UK
Witnesses: The Pritchard
family

THE EVENTS

Marie clutched her husband Vic's hand. A chill ran down her spine as she, Vic and their friend Mr. O'Donald stepped into the dark hallway of her sister Jean Pritchard's haunted house.

Marie switched on a light, terrified of what she might see. What lay before her eyes was just as her nephew Philip had described it...

Dust and water

Philip, aged 15, and his grandmother, were staying in the house alone. All the other members of the family were away.

Earlier that night, Philip had rushed across the road to Marie's house, saying that the living room was filled with strange white dust. Even his grandmother was covered in it. There was also water all over the floor.

Something strange

At first, Marie thought he must have gone crazy, but when she went to see for herself, she realized that Philip was right. Something very strange indeed was going on.

A plant pot was flung violently from the bottom of the stairs to the top, spilling soil everywhere.

In Jean Pritchard's house, Marie found a mysterious, fine white dust had settled all over the furniture in the living room.

A wardrobe began to move. It swayed and tottered like a drunken old man, terrifying the witnesses.

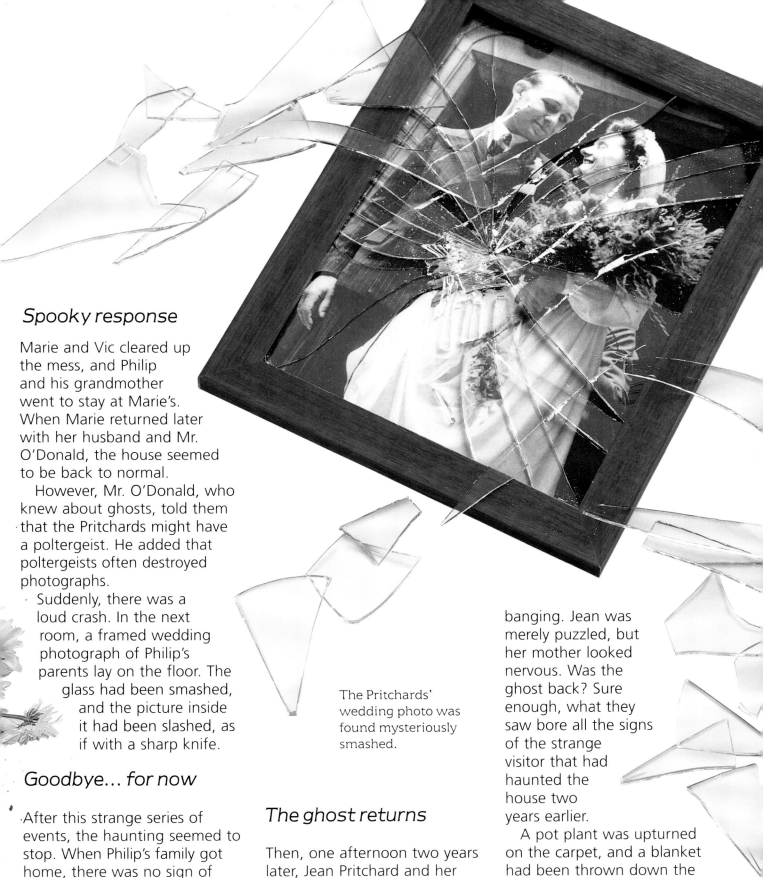

Spooky response

Marie and Vic cleared up the mess, and Philip and his grandmother went to stay at Marie's. When Marie returned later with her husband and Mr. O'Donald, the house seemed to be back to normal.

However, Mr. O'Donald, who knew about ghosts, told them that the Pritchards might have a poltergeist. He added that poltergeists often destroyed photographs.

Suddenly, there was a loud crash. In the next room, a framed wedding photograph of Philip's parents lay on the floor. The glass had been smashed, and the picture inside it had been slashed, as if with a sharp knife.

The Pritchards' wedding photo was found mysteriously smashed.

Goodbye... for now

After this strange series of events, the haunting seemed to stop. When Philip's family got home, there was no sign of anything odd, and nothing else scary happened – for a while.

The ghost returns

Then, one afternoon two years later, Jean Pritchard and her mother were having tea in the kitchen when they heard banging. Jean was merely puzzled, but her mother looked nervous. Was the ghost back? Sure enough, what they saw bore all the signs of the strange visitor that had haunted the house two years earlier.

A pot plant was upturned on the carpet, and a blanket had been thrown down the stairs. This time, however, the spook was here to stay...

Case study 4: PONTEFRACT PANIC

Before long, the Pritchards' house became nightmarish to live in. There were constant banging and crashing noises.

A paintbrush that was being used to paint a bedroom was flung through the air.

The family had objects thrown at them, and huge teeth marks appeared in food that had been left in the refrigerator. In one room, which was being decorated, a roll of wallpaper stood on its end, swaying like a cobra.

The poltergeist seemed to focus on Diane, Philip's younger sister. She was thrown out of bed several times, and dragged up the stairs by her cardigan.

Diane was dragged by an invisible hand.

Candlestick chiller

Eventually, the frightened family called in a priest. The clergyman came to visit the Pritchards, but he was cynical. He told them he didn't believe their stories. If their furniture was moving, he said, it must be caused by the ground subsiding, or caving in, under the house.

At once, as if to prove him wrong, a candlestick floated into the air and moved toward him until it was right under his nose. Then it stopped, and hovered there.

That soon changed the priest's mind. He didn't know what to do, so he left, saying there was evil in the house. The family was as frightened and mystified as ever.

A candlestick seemed to wave itself deliberately in the priest's face.

Aunt Maude comes to stay

Diane's and Philip's Aunt Maude, the sister of their father Joe, didn't believe a word of the poltergeist stories. She thought the children were just playing tricks. So she came to see for herself.

When Maude arrived, all the lights went out. The refrigerator door flew open, and a jug of milk floated out. It crossed the room and poured milk all over Aunt Maude's head!

But Maude still wasn't convinced. She decided to stay the night.

A sleepless night

The night Aunt Maude spent in the house was one of the scariest so far. Crashing noises kept everyone awake; the doors banged, and the entire contents of the refrigerator were flung across the kitchen floor. Then lightbulbs from a room downstairs appeared in the bedroom where Diane, her mother and Aunt Maude were trying to sleep.

Haunting hands

Aunt Maude couldn't deny that something very odd was happening when a lamp floated across the room, all by itself. Then, suddenly, two enormous, hairy hands reached around the half-closed bedroom door. One was at the top, and one near the bottom, so that it looked as if there was a huge monster behind the door. The hands were Aunt Maude's fur gloves, moving all by themselves!

Tune tease

Maude shouted, "Get away – you're evil!" One glove shook its fist at her. Maude then began to sing a hymn to scare the evil away, but the gloves simply beat time to the tune.

Jean Pritchard later admitted that although she was frightened, she had had to smile at the way the ghost was teasing Aunt Maude.

Case study 4: PONTEFRACT PANIC

Menacing monk

At first, the poltergeist that tormented the Pritchard family was invisible. But one night, when Jean and Joe were in bed, their door swung open. There, in the shadows, lurked a tall, cloaked figure. When they switched on the light, however, it vanished.

Several local people said they had seen the figure too. One said the ghostly shape looked like a monk.

Vengeful ghost

The Pritchards had recently discovered that there had once been an old monastery in Pontefract, named St. John's. This was an old Cluniac monastery that had been destroyed in the 16th century.

A local woman thought that the history of the monastery might hold an explanation for the haunting. She said she remembered reading stories about it. One was about a monk who had been hanged for attacking a woman. Could it be possible that his spirit was wandering the Earth, tormenting local people as an act of revenge?

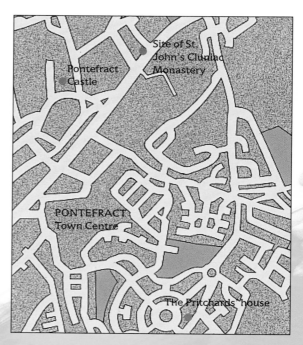

This map shows the location of the Pritchards' house, and the site of the ancient Cluniac monastery that had once stood in the town.

The monk appears... and disappears

One day, Philip and Diane were watching TV when they suddenly saw the monk through a glass door.

Philip ran over to the door, trying to get a better view of the figure. But as he opened the door, the ghost fled.

Philip just managed to see the monk disappear through the kitchen floor. After that, it was never seen again.

Case study 4: THE ASSESSMENT

Is it possible that, as Aunt Maude first thought, the poltergeist activity was actually caused by the Pritchard children playing tricks?

The Pontefract poltergeist was one of the most mischievous ever known. It liked to tease people, which might make it seem like a hoax. However, other poltergeists have been known to tease their victims.

A new focus?

It is very unusual for the same family to have a poltergeist twice. Did a ghost really visit the Pritchards on two different occasions, over a period of two whole years?

The first haunting began when Philip was 15. The ghost then returned when Diane was 14. These are both typical ages for a poltergeist victim. Experts might say that the two teenagers in turn became focuses[1] for a poltergeist.

Was it a monk?

A researcher interested in the case, Colin Wilson, tried to track down the story of the hanged monk. The woman who claimed to have read the story was convinced that she had found it in a book at the local library.

But despite a thorough search, Wilson found no evidence that a monk had ever been hanged in the area. In fact, the monk story seems to have been no more than hearsay, developed into a theory by the Pritchards and their friends.

Seeing things

Apparitions, or visible ghosts, do sometimes occur in poltergeist cases. But that doesn't mean the Pritchards were being haunted by the ghost of a monk.

The Pontefract poltergeist often seemed to respond to people's suggestions. For example, the wedding photograph was smashed shortly after Mr. O'Donald had mentioned photos.

Perhaps, if there really was a poltergeist, it responded to the family's expectations by appearing in the form of a ghost.

No answer

There are many aspects of this case that still baffle researchers. No one has ever explained how Maude's gloves appeared to become a pair of scary hands, or how objects in the house moved around of their own accord.

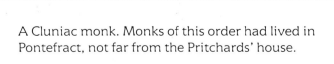

A Cluniac monk. Monks of this order had lived in Pontefract, not far from the Pritchards' house.

[1]See pages 14-15

Case study 5: SPIRITS OF BRAZIL

Brazil, in South America, is one of the world's most haunted countries. Here is a selection of mysterious events that have happened there.

Case: A Poltergeist in Guarulhos
Date: April 27th, 1973
Place: Guarulhos, Sao Paulo, Brazil
Witnesses: Multiple witnesses

THE EVENTS

Noemia was furious. Someone, or something, had carved four long, deep slashes into one of the mattresses in her house.

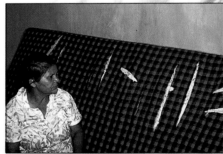

Noemia surveys a mattress which was slashed open, as if with a sharp knife.

At first, she suspected one of her children. But they denied it. When more slashes appeared in sofas, armchairs and curtains, Noemia and her husband, Marcos, were completely baffled.

Invisible blades

One day, three members of the family were together in a bedroom. They stared in horror as, before their eyes, deep cuts appeared in one of the beds.

Monster claw

The next strange experience happened to Pedro, Marcos's father. He was terrified when a monstrous arm appeared before him in the air. Its long, razor-sharp claws reached threateningly toward his face.

A friend visited to see what was going on – but fainted in fright when she saw a huge, long-fingered hand.

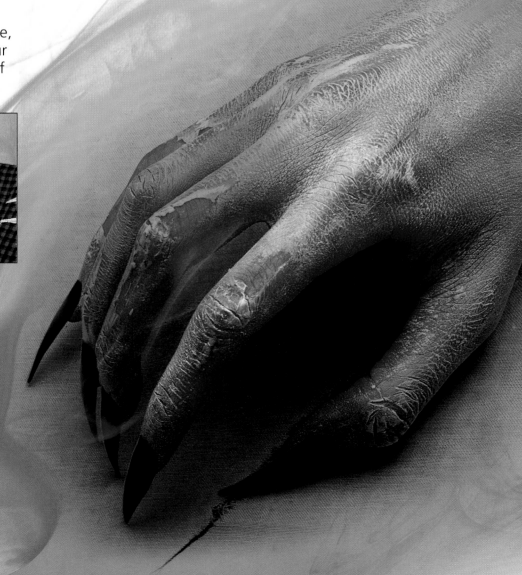

In the flesh

The worst was yet to come. Soon, the ghost began to attack people. One day, Marcos woke in agonizing pain. He looked down in horror at his arm. It was slashed open and was bleeding over everything.

Noemia too was attacked by an invisible presence. Feeling a sudden pain, she looked in the mirror and found tiny, sharp cuts on her face and neck.

Face fright

A few days later, Noemia had another terrifying experience. She had seen vague shapes and shadows before, but this time she clearly caught sight of a grotesque face, with huge fangs, surrounded by flickering flames. Soon afterward, fires started in the house.

The appearance of the horrible fiery face terrified Noemia.

No escape

The evil force followed the petrified family from place to place. They moved a total of six times in an attempt to escape – and each time the poltergeist came with them. It only left in October 1976, after the family decided to hold an exorcism[1].

Did the fierce claws that Pedro saw slash the furniture?

This map shows the sites in Brazil described in case study 5.

Case study 5: SPIRITS OF BRAZIL

Case: Fires in Ramos
Date: 1989
Place: Ramos, Brazil
Witnesses: Multiple witnesses

A fiery devil haunted Sara in her dreams.

THE EVENTS

Sara shrank back in terror. A hideous devil was looming over her, leering and pointing. Laughing evilly, he promised to burn her to death. Sara screamed and buried her face in the bedclothes.

She ran to her grandmother's room, still tormented by her nightmare. When they returned to Sara's bedroom, they froze. The bed was covered in black scorch marks. Someone had tried to start a fire.

Sara and her grandmother were scared by the mysterious burns on the bed.

Flaring up

The trouble had started the day before. After an argument with her grandmother, several small fires had broken out, always near 13-year-old Sara. At first it seemed to be a coincidence.

Explosive

After Sara's nightmare, however, the fires got worse. A mattress, a bundle of clothes and even a damp towel caught fire with loud explosions.

A priest advised the terrified girl to leave the house. She went to stay with a friend, and the fires stopped – but as soon as she returned, they started again.

Cured with kindness

At last, Sara moved in with a kind woman next door, Mrs. de Sousa, and the trouble ended as quickly as it had begun. It seemed that all the strange happenings had been caused by the bad relationship between Sara and her grandmother.

Could it be possible that the fires were started by a poltergeist, expressing Sara's emotions for her with explosive force?

THE EVENTS

It had been a terrible night for 11-year-old Maria. The strange events that had started to happen around her were taking a turn for the worse. Whatever it was that was haunting her, it had definitely become more aggressive.

Maria had awoken during the night when her pillow was pressed against her face, stopping her breathing.

Morning came, and Maria woke again – but she now found that her arm was in total agony.

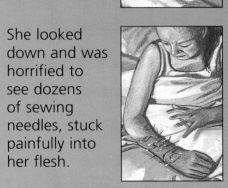

She looked down and was horrified to see dozens of sewing needles, stuck painfully into her flesh.

Ghostly gifts

The haunting hadn't always been so frightening. It had started when falling bricks had appeared from nowhere. Instead of being afraid, Maria accepted the events, and even asked the ghost for presents. If she requested food, it would appear. Once, she asked for a brooch. It appeared at her feet.

Revenge of the dead?

Then the spirit had stopped being so friendly. It started to break things in the house. Crockery was smashed, furniture was hurled around and pictures were knocked from the walls. Maria was slapped and bitten, and the frightening nocturnal attacks began. One day, while she was at school, her clothes suddenly caught fire.

A neighbour, Volpe, took Maria to a Spiritualist club, where mediums tried to contact the ghost.

Volpe watched, amazed, as an eerie spirit voice spoke from Maria's throat. In a past life, it said, Maria had been a witch. Now, the ghost of one of her victims was taking its revenge.

After Maria's visit to the Spiritualists, much of the poltergiest activity stopped. Or so it seemed.

Stones and pieces of brick fell with no warning when Maria was nearby.

A medium from Brazil

A tragic end

Several years later, Maria drank a soft drink which had been laced with poison. She died that day. Could it be suicide? Or murder? Or had a ghost poisoned her, as a last act of vengeance?

The poltergeists of Brazil certainly seem to have scared those who experienced them. But many of these odd and disturbing cases could have a rational explanation.

Monsters in the mind

In the Guarulhos case, Pedro was sure he had seen a hideous claw. But he could have imagined it. Perhaps his mind created an image of a creature that could have made the slashes in the furniture. No one else saw the same claw. Pedro's story could then have scared the other occupants of the house into imagining that they too could see horrible monsters.

Poltergeist poisoning

It seems likely that a living person murdered Maria in the Jabuticabal case, but it is possible that she was poisoned by a spirit. There is a case in which a spirit known as the "Bell Witch" haunted the Bell family in the USA in 1817. The witch's spirit claimed to have killed the father of the family, John Bell. It revealed that it had replaced his medicine bottle with a flask full of poisonous liquid. Bell drank from it, and died. The spirit was apparently delighted at what it had done.

Spontaneous fires

Fires have often been reported in poltergeist cases, although they usually do very little damage.

Perhaps the fires that plagued 13-year-old Sara at Ramos were linked to another type of paranormal event, called Spontaneous Human Combustion, or SHC.

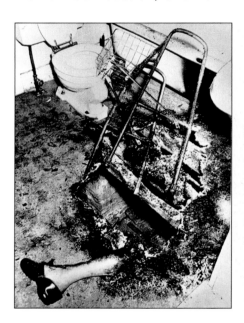

In this famous case of SHC, a leg was all that was left of Dr. J. Irving Bentley after he burst into flames.

In cases of SHC, people themselves burst into flames, without an obvious cause. In Sara's case, however, fires seemed to burn around her, but she herself remained unharmed by them.

Scientists are still trying to explain SHC, and as yet they have not succeeded. The cause of Sara's spontaneous fires also remains a mystery.

SPIRITS OF THE DEAD

Could poltergeists be the spirits of dead people, returning to Earth as spirits? After all, they seem to use rapping, messages or voices to reveal a particular identity from beyond the grave.

Messages, such as this one from Enfield (see page 10), sometimes appear in poltergeist cases.

I WILL STAY IN THIS HOUSE

Questions and answers

Researchers have found that poltergeists often do exactly what observers expect. If people ask them questions, they frequently reply. But this doesn't mean poltergeists are dead spirits. They could be caused by the human mind – or they could be hoaxes.

Days of the Dead

In many Latin American countries, there is a celebration for the dead each November. Families make model skeletons and skulls, and prepare feasts for dead relatives and friends.

The celebrations are happy and festive, not scary. But they do reveal a strong belief in dead spirits in Latin America. This may be why so many ghosts and poltergeists are reported there. If more people believe in ghosts, they are more likely to put unexplained events down to ghostly spirits.

Skeletons, candles and flowers decorate homes.

Decorations based on the theme of skeletons and witches

CHAPTER TWO: ESP?

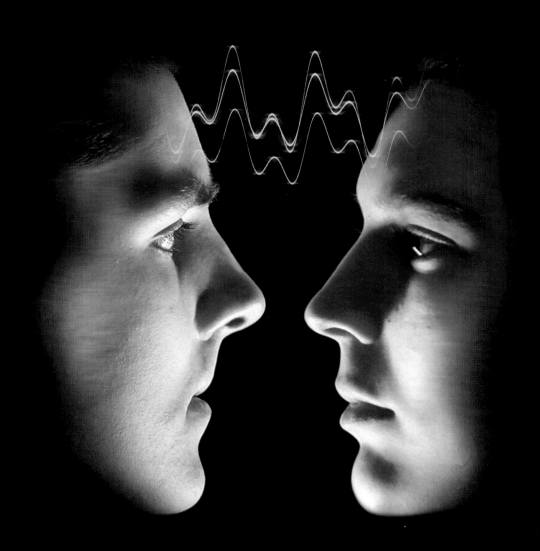

WHAT IS ESP?

Have you ever "known" that a friend was about to telephone you, or had a dream which later came true? If you have, you may have experienced ESP, or extrasensory perception. ESP is a general term for a number of different phenomena. There are specific names for these, which you will come across as you read this chapter.

Telepathy

Telepathy means direct communication between minds. It might be a message sent between just two people, or several people. A simple example of telepathy is somehow knowing that a friend is on their way to see you.

Clairvoyance

Clairvoyance is when someone "sees" information about an object or event, without receiving this information from another person's mind. It means, literally, "clear seeing". An example of clairvoyance would be visualizing where to find a lost set of keys, when no one else knows where they are.

However, the word clairvoyance is often used more generally. When someone is called a clairvoyant, they usually claim to have telepathic powers, and the power to see into the future as well.

Premonitions

A premonition is a warning about something bad that is going to happen in the future. This might be in the form of a dream, a vision, or even just a feeling. It is similar to precognition, which just means seeing the future without it necessarily being bad.

Dowsing

Dowsing is a method of finding something using sticks or rods called dowsing rods. The rods move in the dowser's hands, when he stands on the right spot (field dowsing) or when the rods are over the right spot on a map (map dowsing). Some people believe that dowsing rods are simply tools for focusing the mind's ESP.

Crisis apparitions

Crisis apparitions are a kind of vision, of particular people, or of whole situations. As the name suggests, they tend to be connected to a major crisis of some sort. A crisis apparition may seem to be a sort of ghost, but the vision represents someone who is still alive or only at the point of death, not someone who has been dead for some time.

Being psychic

The term psychic is used to describe someone who experiences any kind of ESP on a regular basis. For most people, psychic experiences happen unexpectedly and are usually a one-off. Psychics, however, often claim that they can use their powers more or less whenever they choose to.

ESP and science

ESP is easier to test for than other paranormal phenomena, because it involves people rather than other beings. As a result, many experiments have been carried out to discover whether it really exists. In this chapter, there is information about how testing began, and how successful the tests have been so far.

Case study 6: ARCTIC EXPEDITION

Date: 1937
Place: New York, USA;
the Arctic

Harold Sherman, who stayed in New York

THE EVENTS

If a person was lost in the Arctic without a radio, would he be able to get help by sending thoughts across the icy wastelands?

One evening in 1937, a famous explorer, Sir Hubert Wilkins, was in a club in New York. He was approached by a writer named Harold Sherman, who asked him exactly this question.

Wilkins was about to start an expedition to look for a crashed plane in the Arctic. The two men chatted about the communication problems he might have, and joked about how telepathy would be the perfect solution. Then the idea dawned on them: why not use this opportunity to see if they could communicate by telepathy?

Sir Hubert Wilkins, the famous explorer, on expedition in the Arctic

Devising a test

They came up with the following experiment: three nights a week, between 11:30pm and midnight, New York time, Wilkins would send mental impressions of his day to Sherman. At the same time, Sherman would write down whatever thoughts came into his mind. He would then send a copy to a researcher named Dr. Gardner Murphy, who would give it to a lawyer for safe keeping. Wilkins would also keep a detailed record of his experiences. When he got back to New York, the two accounts would be put together and compared.

Vivid impressions

In total, there were 68 telepathy sessions, during which Sherman received many strikingly vivid images of the expedition. There was one of an Eskimo funeral, one of Wilkins' plane, and another of a road next to a river.

Another impression was that of a fire. Was it a fire on the ice? The image became clearer, and he saw it was a white house near Wilkins' camp, burning fiercely. People were gathered around it, staring. The flames shot up in the freezing cold air while a sharp wind blew.

Sherman saw a vision of a white house on fire.

One night Sherman had an impression of Wilkins drinking unusual wine.

Another image was of people playing table tennis.

An unlikely evening

Another impression was of a dramatic series of events. Sherman felt that Wilkins' plane had been caught in a snowstorm on his way north, and that he was forced to land at a place named Regina. This in itself was quite likely.

Next, however, he had an image of Wilkins at a ball – in full evening dress. This seemed unbelievable for a man on an Arctic expedition. But Sherman could even see a room full of men and women, so he wrote down his impressions.

On Wilkins' return, Sherman's impressions were put to the test.

Case study 6: ARCTIC EXPEDITION

Amazing results

The results of the experiment were stunning. Time and time again, Sherman's impressions had been right. The most amazing account of all was the story about the ball. The account below, based on Wilkins' log book, shows how accurate Sherman's version was:

This morning took off on flight. Hoping to reach Saskatchewan. Was caught in heavy blizzard. Propose to turn back and land in Regina.

Was met at the airport by the Governor of the province who invited me to attend an officers' ball being held there that evening.

As I did not have suitable clothing with me, my attendance at this ball was made possible by the loan to me of an evening dress suit.

On route to the Arctic, Wilkins was forced to stay in Regina because of the treacherous weather conditions.

Matching details

Many of Sherman's other impressions were also correct. The fire he had seen turned out to be an Eskimo's shack burning. Members of the expedition had played table tennis in a school gym one evening, and one evening Wilkins had tried blueberry wine. There had been an Eskimo child's funeral on the day that Sherman specified.

HOW TO MAKE ESP
EXTRASENSORY PERCEPTION
WORK FOR YOU
All of us have within us an incredible mental power that can change our lives overnight. If you are ready to explore this miraculous dimension of your mind, read this book!
HAROLD SHERMAN
FAWCETT 0-449-21202-5

The astounding results deeply affected Harold Sherman. As a result, he devoted his life to psychic research and wrote several books about ESP.

Case study 6: THE ASSESSMENT

This experiment seems to be a classic demonstration of telepathy at work. There seems little doubt that the two accounts were similar. But could there be any other explanations?

 Inaccuracies

The impressions Sherman received were not completely accurate. He got a number of things wrong. For example, he thought that the Eskimo funeral was for an adult, not a child, and he pictured the shack fire 800km (500 miles) from where it really happened. Also, before his return to New York, Wilkins went on one last major flight to look for the crashed plane. Sherman failed to pick up any impressions at all of this.

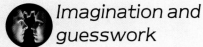 **Imagination and guesswork**

Many images which Sherman described were of local people and landscapes. Sherman was a writer, and probably very imaginative. This, together with the fact that he must have had a good idea of what the Arctic was like, could explain many of his impressions. However, it is still difficult to explain the more unusual incidents, or the times when the dates for each event apparently matched up in the two accounts.

 Did the men cheat?

The fact that the experiment was monitored by other people would have made cheating difficult. Sherman could, perhaps, have received information from another member of the expedition. This is unlikely, as little information was available about the expedition until it was over.

Cheating is also unlikely because both men were well-known and respected, and neither would have wanted to spoil his reputation.

All in the interpretation?

Both men believed in ESP and wanted their experiment to succeed, so they may have read too much into the similarities between the accounts.

It is unclear what happened to the original diary and log book. What is known is that Sherman wrote pages and pages, probably far more than Wilkins wrote in his log book. The men may have picked out the parts of Sherman's account that matched the log book, then interpreted other slight similarities as successes as well.

The shack fire happened at Point Barrow, not Aklavik, as Sherman thought.

COINCIDENCE

Imagine being in a foreign country and unexpectedly bumping into someone you haven't seen for years. What would you think? Would you think that it had happened completely by chance, or that it had happened for a reason?

Different perspectives

A coincidence is when two or more unrelated things connect unexpectedly. It's the word that people use when they believe these events have happened by chance.

Some people think that very few events are coincidences. They believe that there has to be a reason for the strange connections that happen in life. Some think that ESP can explain many seemingly coincidental events – if we are all communicating with each other telepathically, we may be able to influence each other's actions as well.

Other people think that unlikely events are bound to happen every now and again.

Research findings

Research has shown that we find it hard to believe when coincidences happen to us personally; but we are less surprised when they happen to other people. We can see how chance works in the world around us, but we like to think that our personal experiences are somehow special.

Coincidence – or the powers of ESP?

This event is a good example of something very unlikely. It actually happened on a London Underground train in 1971.

A passenger suddenly pressed the emergency button to stop the train. Strangely, the train was already stopping.

What the passenger didn't know was that someone had just thrown himself in front of the train. The train driver saw him jump, and stopped the train just in time.

The passenger couldn't say why he had pressed the emergency button. Was it just a coincidence?

Once inside the train, the passenger wouldn't have been able to see anything happening in front of it – but it's possible that he knew by ESP that the train should stop.

The train driver would have braked suddenly when he saw the man jump. Could the sudden braking have caused the passenger to panic and press the button?

Case study 7: PSYCHIC DETECTIVES

If ESP really exists, we may be able to use it to trace people, exchange news, or even to solve crimes.

Case: The Stolen Painting
Date: 1974
Place: London, UK

THE EVENTS

Nella Jones

In 1974, a famous painting called *The Guitar Player* by Vermeer was stolen from the gallery of Kenwood House in London. When psychic detective Nella Jones heard the news, a mysterious map-like picture began to form in her mind.

The Guitar Player by Vermeer was taken out of its frame by the thieves.

"X" marks the spot

Nella sketched the picture and marked two crosses on it. She phoned the police and told them exactly where to find the picture frame. They followed her directions, and found it. Then she said that a lake near Kenwood held some more evidence. Indeed, the police found the picture's alarm mechanism at the edge of the water, where the thieves had thrown it.

Next, Nella told them that the picture would be found in a cemetery, unharmed. To their complete amazement, this also turned out to be true.

Was she guilty?

The police were so astonished at the accuracy of Nella's information that they wondered if she had been involved in the theft herself. When they found the real thieves, however, they cleared her name.

Kenwood House, the site of the crime

Case study 7: PSYCHIC DETECTIVES

> Case: The Yorkshire
> Ripper
> Date: The late 1970s
> Place: Yorkshire, UK

THE EVENTS

Nella Jones's reputation grew over the next few years. When, in the 1970s, a man known as the Yorkshire Ripper was carrying out gruesome murders of women in Northern England, Nella came forward again.

Nella made many claims about the Ripper. For over a year, she gave impressions of who he was and what he did.

Nella claimed that particular letters, names and numbers came into her mind when she thought of the Ripper.

She said he was a truck driver, and that his name was Peter. She saw the letter C painted on the side of his truck, and said that he lived in Bradford. Nella even claimed to know what number house he lived in – number six. She predicted that he would murder someone with the initials J.H., and said he would strike again on November 17th or 27th, 1980.

Nella thought she could sense the name Peter.

The Ripper's arrest

On November 17th, 1980, the Ripper claimed his last victim, just as Nella had predicted. The woman's name was Jaqueline Hill.

After a mammoth police search, the Ripper was finally arrested in January 1981. His name was Peter Sutcliffe, and he was indeed a truck driver, working for a company called T. & W.H. Clark. He lived in Bradford, and his address was 6 Garden Lane.

Peter Sutcliffe, the Yorkshire Ripper, on his wedding day

THE EVENTS

In 1958, the police in Miami, Florida contacted a psychic named Peter Hurkos. A taxi cab driver had been shot, and the police were at a loss for clues.

The police took Hurkos to the cab, and he sat inside. He absorbed the atmosphere, touching the steering wheel and the dashboard.

Impressions soon began to form in his mind as he sat in the cab. The killer was tall and slim, and came from Detroit; he had a tattoo; his friends called him Smitty.

Hurkos claimed to receive information through his hands.

Then Hurkos dropped a bombshell. He announced that this wasn't the only murder. He was sure there had been another. The murderer had killed someone else, recently, in Key West, another part of Florida.

Matching bullets

The police checked with their colleagues in Key West. Hurkos was absolutely right; another man had been shot, and the bullets in his body were from the same gun as those found in the cab driver's body.

The Miami police worked on the details that Hurkos had given them, and contacted their colleagues in Detroit. They managed to piece

Peter Hurkos

together enough information to lead them to a man named Charles Smith. He was arrested and went to trial, where he was found guilty of both murders.

Case study 7: PSYCHIC DETECTIVES

Case: The Boston
Strangler
Date: 1962-1964
Place: Boston, USA

THE EVENTS

When a number of women
were horrifically strangled in
Boston, the police had a
desperate search on their hands
for the killer. After hunting with
no success, they decided to call
in Peter Hurkos again.

Hurkos let his mind run
free as he touched the
scarves and
stockings.

The police
showed Hurkos
photos of the crimes,
along with stockings
and scarves that had
belonged to the victims.
Hurkos studied the photos
and touched the scarves and
stockings. Very quickly, he
began to build a picture of
the murderer.

Using touch in
this way is
known as
psychometry
(see page 54).

Conflicting views

Hurkos claimed that the
murderer was fairly short, had
a pointed nose, a scar on his
left arm, and that he used to
work with diesel engines.
Hurkos himself believed a shoe
salesman to be the Strangler.
However, after a long hunt,
the police decided that they
didn't agree with him. A
schizophrenic named Albert De
Salvo confessed to the crimes,
and the police accepted his
confession.

Albert De Salvo being escorted by a
police officer following his arrest

Mistaken identity?

De Salvo fitted the description
Hurkos had given to the police.
He had a pointed nose, a scar
on his arm and he used to
work with diesel engines. Yet
Hurkos still insisted that the
shoe salesman was the real
culprit. Who was right? De
Salvo's mental health was too
poor for him to go on trial, so
the police never proved he was
the killer.
After his arrest, however,
the horrific activities
of the Strangler
came to a stop.

Case study 7: THE ASSESSMENT

Whenever there is a dramatic crime or series of crimes, police detectives are often approached by psychics offering help. This can cause more problems than it solves. Valuable police time is used to follow up suggestions, which often turn out to be worthless. However, Nella Jones and Peter Hurkos have both been praised by some police officers for their help.

Hit and miss

One of the problems faced by the police is that psychic information is often hit and miss. For example, Nella was apparently very precise when she located the stolen painting, but she was a lot less precise about the Ripper. She suggested the name Peter, but she also suggested Harry, Charles and Leonard. She was right about his house number, but she thought his street was called Chapel Street. She also claimed, wrongly, that the Ripper would strike again after the murder of Jaqueline Hill.

Too vague?

Although the Miami police found Hurkos helpful in the cab driver case, the Boston police were clearly not so sure about his views on the Boston Strangler. If anything, the disagreement showed that the sort of information he could give was too vague – it could apply to too many people.

Psychic technique

Nella Jones admitted to some of the wrong guesses that she made about the Ripper. It's unusual, however, for psychics to do this. Research has shown that psychics often work by making many guesses; if they make enough, some are bound to be right. They then emphasize the right ones and downplay the wrong ones (people aren't interested in wrong guesses, anyway). They are also helped by the fact that major crimes are covered in a sensational way by the media, who are only too ready to listen to a psychic's claims.

Psychic detectives often benefit from media coverage, such as the newspaper stories shown here.

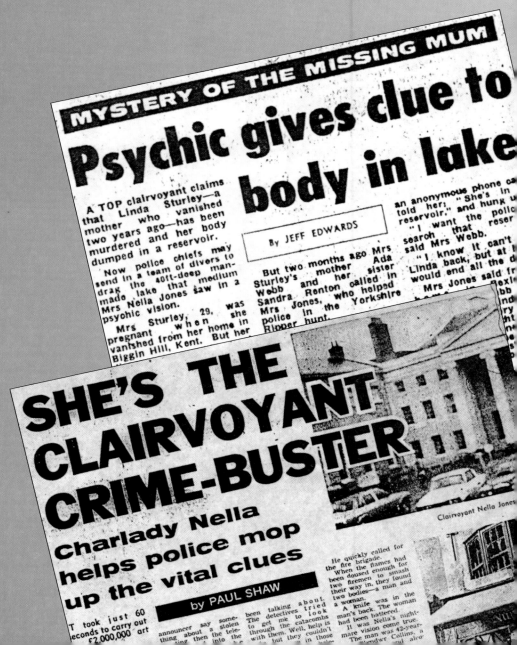

MYSTERY OF THE MISSING MUM

Psychic gives clue to body in lake

BY JEFF EDWARDS

A TOP clairvoyant claims that Linda Sturley—a mother who vanished two years ago—has been murdered and her body dumped in a reservoir.

Now police chiefs may send in a team of divers to drag the 40ft-deep man-made lake that medium Mrs Nella Jones saw in a psychic vision.

Mrs Sturley, 29, was pregnant when she vanished from her home in Biggin Hill, Kent. But her ...

But two months ago Mrs Sturley's mother Ada Webb and her sister Sandra Renton called in Mrs Jones, who helped police in the Yorkshire Ripper hunt.

an anonymous phone ca... told her: "She's in ... reservoir," and hung u... "I want the polic... search that reser... said Mrs Webb. "I know it can't ... Linda back, but at l... would end all the d... Mrs Jones said fr...

SHE'S THE CLAIRVOYANT CRIME-BUSTER

Charlady Nella helps police mop up the vital clues

by PAUL SHAW

...T took just 60 seconds to carry out £2,000,000 art ... announcer say some-thing about a stolen ... then the tele-... into the ...

...been talking about. The detectives tried to get me to look through the catacombs with them. Well, help is ... but they couldn't ... in those ...

He quickly called for the fire brigade. When the flames had been doused enough for two firemen to smash their way in, they found two bodies—a man and a woman.

A knife was in the man's back. The woman had been battered ... It was Nella's night-mare vision come true. The man was 42-year...

Clairvoyant Nella Jones

ESP – HISTORY AND SCIENCE

Ancient records show that people have believed in psychic experiences, such as premonitions, for thousands of years. However, terms such as ESP and telepathy have not existed very long. They were only invented as interest in psychic happenings grew.

A 19th-century obsession

In the 19th century, many people in Europe and America claimed to have psychic experiences. The more people talked about them, the more they seemed to happen.

At first, most of the claims were about contacting the spirit world, and so the obsession became known as Spiritualism[1]. As the craze grew, however, Spiritualism came to include other phenomena, such as hypnotizing people, levitating, which means rising and floating in the air, and reading people's minds.

Serious investigation

By the 1880s, many Spiritualists had been shown to be frauds. However, some people started to think that there might sometimes be a scientific explanation for the experiences.

In 1882, a group of Spiritualists and scientists set up the Society for Psychical Research (SPR) in London, to investigate people's claims.

The SPR began to put the different kinds of psychic

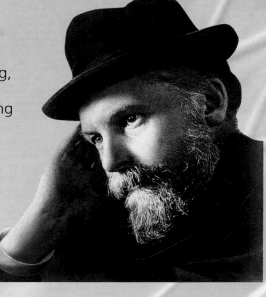

F.W.H. Myers, one of the founders of the SPR, who invented the term "telepathy"

experience into categories. Two of these categories were mind reading and clairvoyance. One of the SPR's founders, F.W.H. Myers, gave mind reading a new name – he called it telepathy.

The SPR also collected thousands of accounts of psychic experiences, many of which were published together in a book called *Phantasms of the Living*.

Finding a test

The SPR's work was significant because, for the first time, psychic experiences were treated rationally.

While the society gathered many interesting stories, however, this was not enough to prove that they had really happened. Early in the 20th century, scientists started to think of ways to test people's psychic ability.

A 19th-century seance. People claimed to contact spirits at meetings like this.

[1]See page 18

Dr. Joseph Rhine

In 1934, a scientist called Dr. Joseph Rhine gave a new name to phenomena such as clairvoyance and telepathy – he called them extrasensory perception, or ESP.

He also developed new ways of testing for them. He realized that ESP could only be proved to exist in strictly monitored experiments. Cheating would have to be completely ruled out, and the results would need to be clearly analyzed.

Dr. Rhine worked in the Parapsychology Laboratory of Duke University, North Carolina, USA

Zener cards

Dr. Rhine often used a pack of cards called Zener cards. In one experiment, he would choose cards at random and ask the "subject" (the person being tested for ESP) to guess which he had chosen. For the experiment to work, he had to show that the subjects guessed the correct cards (known as the "targets") more often than chance could account for.

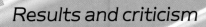

These are the five different symbols in a pack of Zener cards.

Results and criticism

These experiments seemed to succeed in demonstrating ESP, and they attracted a lot of attention. However, when other scientists tried to repeat them, they didn't get the same results. Many began to question whether Dr. Rhine had monitored his experiments strictly enough.

Case study 8: LOST IN THE ANDES

**Date: October -
December, 1972
Place: The Andes,
South America**

THE EVENTS

On October 13th, 1972, a plane went missing high in the Andes mountains in South America. There were 45 young men and women on board. A search was mounted, but there was no sign of the wreck. The passengers' families became frantic with worry. Was there nothing anyone could do?

A difficult flight

The passengers on the plane, a Fairchild F-27, were mainly a rugby team from Montevideo, Uruguay, on their way to play a game in Santiago, Chile. As they had flown through the treacherous Planchon Pass in the Andes, bad weather had shaken the plane. Soon afterwards, however, the pilot thought they had cleared the mountains, and began to descend. Then, suddenly, the rocky mountainside loomed up, dangerously close. The wing of the plane clipped the rocks. It broke off, and the plane crashed down the mountain, breaking into pieces as it went.

After hitting the rocky mountainside, the main body of the plane eventually came to rest on its belly.

This is the route taken by the plane. The weather was too bad to cross straight from Mendoza to Santiago, so the pilot had chosen to fly south to cross the mountains through the Planchon Pass, near Malargue.

Survival

When the main body of the plane came to rest, many passengers were amazed to find that they were still alive and unharmed. Not everyone was so lucky. Some had died instantly, and some had serious injuries. However, of the 45 people on board, over 30 had survived.

The survivors were sure that help would come quickly. They tended to the injured as best they could, gathered together what food they could find among the wreckage and settled down to wait.

A desperate hunt

News that the plane had disappeared reached the passengers' relatives, and the Chilean Air Force Aerial Rescue Service started a search. They hunted for eight days, and found nothing. Then they gave up.

The rescue team's symbol

The relatives were horrified, and couldn't believe the search had ended so soon. What if their loved ones were still alive?

The old dowser

Some of the relatives decided to carry on searching themselves, and went to Chile to hunt for clues.

One woman went to an old dowser in Montevideo, Uruguay, instead. She took a map of the Andes with her. The old man's rods crossed over one area, and the woman noted where it was.

When her daughter, Madelon, gave this information to the other relatives, she was told that the area picked out by the dowser had already been searched by the rescue team. Disappointed, Madelon decided to try someone else.

The main section of the plane in the snow, with a body lying outside it

Case study 8: LOST IN THE ANDES

A famous psychic

Madelon found out about a famous psychic called Gerard Croiset. Unfortunately, he was ill, but his son, also called Gerard Croiset, offered to help as he claimed to have the same psychic abilities as his father. Madelon sent Croiset a map of the Andes and details of everything they knew about the plane's flight path.

Croiset's clues

A few days later, Croiset phoned Madelon. He said he felt that the co-pilot had taken over from the pilot and had been flying the plane alone at the time of the crash, and that the crash had happened 65km (40 miles) from the Planchon Pass. He said he was sure there were survivors.

This gave the searchers renewed hope. One of the parents asked people who lived near the mountain to help hunt for the plane. As the days went by, Croiset sent more impressions. He described how the plane had broken into pieces. It had been heading for water – the sea, or a lake.

The relatives searched the area shown, prompted by Croiset's clues.

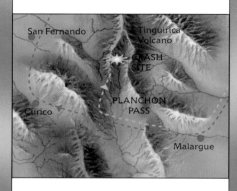

Chilean rescue team's search

The relatives' search

----- Actual flight path

----- Intended flight path

Croiset claimed the plane was near a village of white, Mexican-style houses.

He said the wreckage was hidden under an overhanging rock.

No progress

None of Croiset's clues led the relatives to the plane. After a while, Croiset himself gave up hope. He confessed that he now believed that everyone aboard the plane had died.

Starvation

Up on the mountain, the number of survivors was dwindling. Some had died of their injuries. Others had died when an avalanche swept over them. To make things worse, there was hardly any food left. They had only a few chocolates and some wine. Then they thought of something else – the bodies of the people who had died, preserved in the snow. They could use them for food. At first, this seemed a terrible idea, but as days went by, their hunger grew too great. They began to slice off pieces of human flesh, and eat them.

Plan of escape

Weeks went by, but there was still no sign of a rescue team. The survivors tried climbing down the mountain, but found that it was too difficult because they had become so physically weak. As a result, the strongest among them were chosen to eat more of the human flesh to build up their strength. After several more weeks, they decided it was time to try again.

Success!

Against all the odds, two of the survivors managed the treacherous journey down the mountain, and made contact with some villagers who lived in the valley below. The villagers alerted the rescue services immediately, and before long everyone was brought to safety.

At the end of their incredible ordeal, the survivors had spent 10 long weeks on the mountain. Just 16 of them were left alive.

The two who made it down the mountain being taken to safety.

Some of the survivors with their rescuers at the site of the crash.

Looking back

When the survivors were back home, their relatives assessed their search and where they had gone wrong. Gerard Croiset's clues, they realized, had misled them.

The plane hadn't been heading for water, and neither was it hidden by an overhanging rock; and Croiset had been wrong when he decided that all the survivors had died.

The plane had, however, broken into pieces as he had described, and there was a village that had white houses nearby.

The man they ignored

One person had got the location of the plane right. He was the old dowser from Montevideo that Madelon had consulted. He had located the plane almost exactly.

If the relatives had followed his advice, there might have been more survivors, and their terrible ordeal would have been over so much sooner.

Case study 8: THE ASSESSMENT

This case study shows some of the difficulties and dangers in using ESP as a means of gaining information. Even when some psychic impressions may turn out to be accurate in the end, they can be very difficult to interpret when they are first received.

 ### The person who got it right

There is little doubt that the old water dowser in Montevideo hit upon the plane's location. As with most successes of this sort, it could be dismissed as a coincidence. However, what's certain is that some of the relatives of the crash victims wished they had taken more notice of what he had to say.

 ### Croiset's guesses

Gerard Croiset's successes seem likely to have been lucky guesses, because so many of his suggestions turned out to be wide of the mark.

Sceptics often point to the fact that if a psychic makes enough guesses, some of them are bound to be right.

Knowledge of events

It is perhaps not really surprising that Croiset thought he saw images such as the plane breaking up, or its remains hidden under a rock. Given that the plane had undoubtedly crashed, either possibility would be easy to imagine.

Psychometry

Gerard Croiset used a psychic technique known as psychometry. The psychic receives insight about a situation by touching objects that are connected with it – in this particular case, maps of the region.

The original idea of psychometry was developed by a scientist named J. R. Buchanan, in the 1830s. He suggested that objects record events or emotions, then transmit the information in some way.

Today, most psychometrists use objects simply to trigger their psychic powers. In other words, the power is believed to be in the psychic's mind, not in the object itself.

Psychometrists use their hands as a psychic tool.

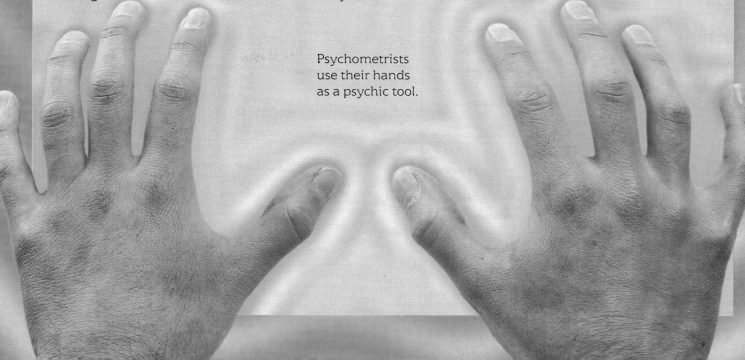

Case study 9: THE RICH AND FAMOUS

ESP often seems to be triggered by traumatic or tragic events. Few deaths are as dramatic as the sudden death of a young, famous person, so it may not be surprising that several are associated with accounts of psychic experience.

Case: Princess Diana
Date: August 31st, 1997
Place: Paris, France

THE EVENTS

Early in the morning on August 31st, 1997, an incredible piece of news hit the headlines: Diana, Princess of Wales, had been killed in a terrible car crash in Paris.

The site of the fatal crash in Paris

Princess Diana was in the prime of life, with a glittering future ahead of her. She was probably the most famous woman in the world, and was followed everywhere by the media. People all over the world were deeply shaken. It seemed incredible that someone like her could be killed so suddenly.

However, there was one woman who wasn't at all surprised to hear the news. In fact, it was exactly what she'd been expecting.

Clairvoyant

Earlier in 1997, the chairman of the British UFO Research Association (BUFORA), Steve Gamble, was contacted by a woman who claimed to have had premonitions and wanted Steve to document them properly.

A lengthy interview

They met on the weekend of August 24th, 1997, and Steve wrote down all the woman's predictions. Some of them were about events which had already happened, so it was impossible for Steve to check her story. However, one of her predictions was that Diana, Princess of Wales would die in a car crash within a year, and possibly sooner – within one or two months. To Steve's amazement, it was only a week before the prediction came true.

Diana, Princess of Wales. Most people were shocked by her death.

Case: James Dean
Date: September 23rd, 1955
Place: Hollywood, USA

THE EVENTS

In 1955, the actor James Dean was at the start of a great career. His first film, *East of Eden*, had been an instant hit, and his next, *Rebel Without a Cause*, made him a teenage idol. He lived an exciting life, and loved driving around in fast cars.

The Porsche Spider

In September 1955, James Dean bought a new sports car. It was sleek, stylish, and very powerful – a Porsche Spider. Excited by his purchase, James began to show it off to his friends. On September 23rd, he met fellow actor Alec Guinness in a restaurant.

Instant foreboding

Alec agreed to go outside to look at the car. The minute he saw the car he turned to James and said, "Please never get in it. It is now 10 o'clock Friday, September 23rd, 1955. If you get in that car you will be found dead in it by this time next week."

The horrific state of James Dean's Porsche Spider after the crash

James ignored Alec's request. He was far too excited about driving the Porsche to worry about what his friend had said. But the following Friday, almost exactly a week later, James did indeed meet his end. He had a horrendous crash in the Porsche and died instantly.

James next to the famous Porsche Spider

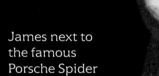

Case: John F. Kennedy
Date: November 22nd, 1963
Place: Dallas, Texas, USA

THE EVENTS

Suddenly, as United States President John F. Kennedy was driven through the streets of Dallas, shots rang out. The president slumped forward. The marksman, whoever he was, had hit the spot. One bullet had hit the president's head, another his neck. He never regained consciousness.

President Kennedy

A popular president

The assassination happened on Friday, November 22nd, 1963. The president had been in office for almost three years, having been voted in on November 9th, 1960. He was popular, and symbolized a new, youthful America. But someone had foreseen that his time in office would end in tragedy – as far back as 1952.

Jeane Dixon's powers

Jeane Dixon was used to seeing visions. One morning in 1952, she was filled with a strange detached feeling, a sure sign that she was about

Jeane Dixon

to foresee something important. Sure enough, she saw the White House, where United States presidents live, with the date 1960 above it. She saw a man with blue eyes and brown hair. Suddenly, she knew that he would become president in 1960. Then she felt something else. It was terrible. This man would be assassinated, during his time in office.

President Kennedy and his wife minutes before the assassination

The day draws near

Eight years later, John F. Kennedy became president. He fitted her vision perfectly. But as time went on, Jeane kept seeing a black cloud, hovering over the White House. Then, on November 22nd, 1963, she knew the fated day had come...

The president's family at his funeral

Case study 9: THE ASSESSMENT

All famous people have one thing in common: other people are interested in their lives and in what will happen to them. This interest may be a major factor in explaining all the celebrity tragedies that have been predicted.

An uncertain future

Princess Diana's future was widely speculated about in the media. People wanted to know as much as possible about her. Would she marry again? Would she remain popular, or would her lifestyle eventually turn people against her?

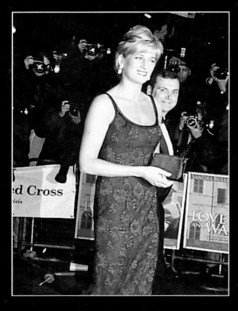

Photographers followed Princess Diana everywhere.

It's therefore not really surprising that out of all the millions of people wondering about her future, one person had the idea that she might die in a car crash.

A likely situation

James Dean's love of speed and fast cars, along with his reckless nature, made him a likely candidate for a car crash.

It's also possible that Alec Guiness's words were given greater significance after James's death. When he saw the powerful car, he may have said something like, "You'll kill yourself in that!" without meaning it literally.

As his words were not recorded, we can't be sure. It's common for people to re-interpret memories after an event. Alec's grief at losing his friend may have led him to believe he had given a more specific warning than he really had.

The young Alec Guinness

Ready for office

A closer look at President Kennedy's life makes Jeane Dixon's predictions less remarkable. His father, a former US Ambassador, had groomed him for office from an early age, so it is not surprising that she predicted he would become president.

His assassination was not so easy to foresee, but it was still not altogether unlikely given the political unrest of the 1950s and 60s in the United States.

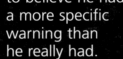

Joseph Kennedy, John F. Kennedy's father

ESP AND IDENTICAL TWINS

Many identical twins claim to know what the other twin is thinking, even when they are apart. But does this suggest that twins are more psychic than other people?

Separate lives

Identical twins Jan and Sue grew up together, but had lived apart for years. Sue married and moved from England to Australia; Jan also married but stayed in England.

A painful event

One day, Jan was at home when she felt a terrible pain in her lower abdomen. She was sure it had something to do with Sue, and told her husband so.

Later that day she phoned her sister in Australia, and Sue's husband answered. He told Jan that Sue had suffered a miscarriage earlier in the day, and had been in a lot of pain, exactly where Jan had been in pain earlier.

Unusual closeness

Identical twins are often brought up to do everything together. Other people – even their parents – are often fascinated by their similarity and actually encourage them to act as one person instead of two. This often leads to a closeness which is beyond most people's experience. As a result, both the twins and the people around them can tend to believe they are psychic.

No firm evidence

This attitude may explain Jan and Sue's story. If Jan was used to linking her experience with Sue's, she might assume that the pain in her abdomen was also linked in this way – but it may have been a coincidence.

In ESP tests, it has been shown that identical twins do tend to think in very similar ways, but that their psychic ability appears to be no higher than anyone else's.

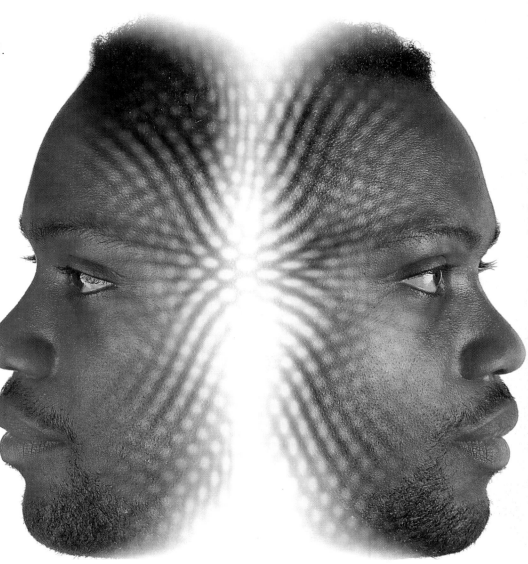

Could twins' minds have a special connection?

Case study 10: CRISIS APPARITIONS

In this case study, there are three accounts of crisis apparitions that all differ in important respects. These differences may give clues as to what the apparitions really are.

Case: A Man at the Door
Date: December 7th, 1918
Place: Near Scampton Airbase, Lincolnshire, UK

THE EVENTS

The date was December 7th, 1918. Two friends in the British Royal Flying Corps met up in the morning at their base in Scampton, Lincolnshire. One of them, Flight Lieutenant David McConnel, was to fly off on a routine mission to Tadcaster, 60 miles (95km) away. His friend, Flight Lieutenant James Larkin, was staying at Scampton.

It was a dull and foggy December day, but the pilots were used to flying in poor weather.

"I'll be back in time for tea," said McConnel.

Back early?

At 3:25pm, Larkin was in his room when McConnel opened the door. He had obviously just got back, because he was still in full flying gear.

"Hallo boy," he said to Larkin.

"Back already?" said Larkin. He was surprised that McConnel had done the trip so quickly, especially in the fog.

"Yes," said McConnel. "Got there all right. Had a good trip."

The friends chatted for a few minutes. Then McConnel said, "Well, cheerio." He shut the door and left.

McConnel stood in the doorway with his hand on the doorknob.

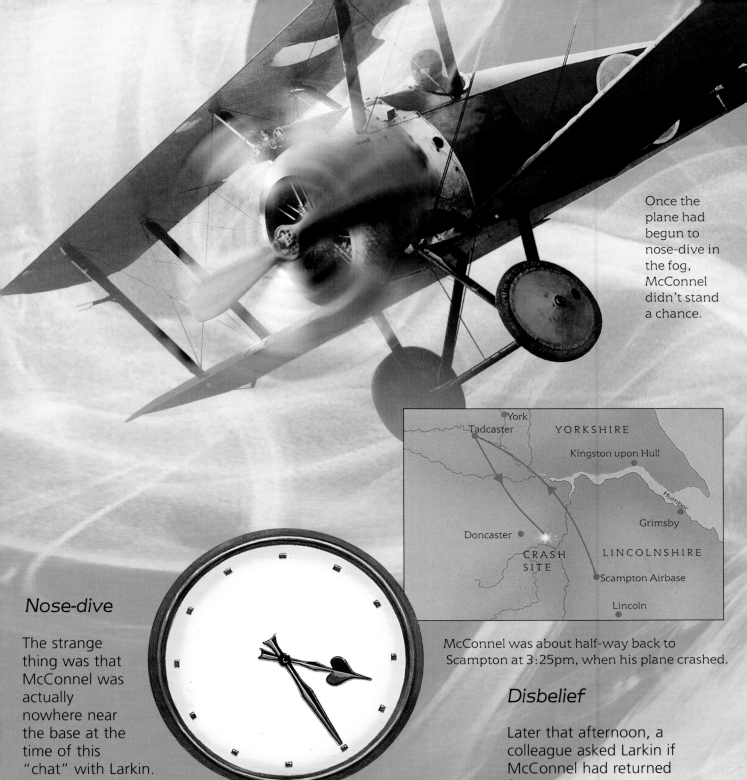

Once the plane had begun to nose-dive in the fog, McConnel didn't stand a chance.

York
Tadcaster
YORKSHIRE
Kingston upon Hull
Humber
Doncaster
Grimsby
CRASH SITE
LINCOLNSHIRE
Scampton Airbase
Lincoln

Nose-dive

The strange thing was that McConnel was actually nowhere near the base at the time of this "chat" with Larkin. He had indeed completed his trip to Tadcaster, and he had started back for the Scampton base. The fog was getting thicker, and he was having trouble seeing through it. He concentrated hard on keeping the plane on course. Then, suddenly, it nose-dived. McConnel tried desperately to bring it back up, but the plane spiralled out of control. There was nothing he could do, and he plummeted to his death in a terrible crash. It was 3:25pm.

McConnel was about half-way back to Scampton at 3:25pm, when his plane crashed.

Disbelief

Later that afternoon, a colleague asked Larkin if McConnel had returned from his trip.

"Yes, he's back," said Larkin. It was only later that evening that he was told the truth – that his friend had been tragically killed in the fog. McConnel couldn't possibly have visited him in his room. Larkin could scarcely believe it.

Case study 10: CRISIS APPARITIONS

Case: Mrs. Collier
Date: January 3rd, 1856
Place: Mississippi
River, USA

THE EVENTS

Mrs. Collier woke up suddenly, her heart pounding. There was someone in her room. A man – standing at the foot of her bed.

"Joseph!" she exclaimed. It was her son. She sat up, horrified. His face! It was so badly cut, and disfigured, and there were bandages all around his head. Why was he there? He should have been in command of a boat on the Mississippi River, far, far away.

Then he disappeared. Mrs. Collier was totally bewildered. What could she have seen?

Mrs. Collier saw Joseph in the first light of dawn, standing at the bottom of her bed.

A fatal collision

It was January 3rd, 1856. Joseph Collier was on board his riverboat, very early in the morning. The sky was still almost dark, although the eastern horizon was growing lighter. Mist hung over the water, and visibility was poor. Joseph stood on deck, directing his crew as they peered into the gloom. The boat moved slowly down the river.

Suddenly, another boat loomed up out of the mist. Joseph desperately shouted orders to his crew, but it was too late. The boats smashed into each other.

A Mississippi riverboat like the one captained by Joseph Collier

The falling mast

The crash broke one of the ship's masts. Joseph saw it too late. The mast fell and knocked him over, crushing his skull and killing him.

Two weeks later, Mrs. Collier heard the tragic news. She remembered her vision of Joseph. It must have appeared just as the mast fell upon him.

Case: Bonnie Mogyorossy
Date: January 1970
Place: Vietnam

THE EVENTS

For Bonnie Mogyorossy, what began as a pleasant evening with friends turned into the night of a chilling vision.

It was the day of the president's annual State of the Union address. Bonnie's fiancé Don was away from the United States, fighting in the Vietnam War, but Bonnie was in a good mood because she had just received a letter from him.

She decided to spend the evening with some friends and watch the president with them. As he began his speech, they settled down in front of the television.

President Nixon giving his State of the Union address in 1970

Nightmare on the screen

Suddenly, Bonnie saw something strange happen on the screen. The president was disappearing, and a jungle scene was appearing instead. Then, to her horror, she saw a person lying on the ground in the middle of the scene. It was Don. It seemed that he had been shot, and a voice pounded through her head, saying,

"He's dead. Don is dead."

The terrifying vision of the Vietnam battlefield was all that Bonnie could see on the screen.

A fit of hysterics

Bonnie burst into an hysterical fit of crying. Her friends turned to her in amazement – a few minutes earlier, she had been perfectly happy. So Bonnie told them what she had seen.

Her friends couldn't believe it, as none of them had seen anything of the sort. They assured her that she must have fallen asleep during the President's speech and dreamed it.

When she had calmed down, Bonnie began to think they might be right, and she tried to forget about it.

Terrible news

A week later, Bonnie received news of Don's death: he had indeed been killed in action.

But the tragic news had an extraordinary twist... it turned out that Don had been killed on the very night that Bonnie had seen him on TV.

Case study 10: THE ASSESSMENT

There are three main schools of thought about crisis apparitions. The first is the sceptical opinion that they are imagined, or invented, by the people who see them.

Another view is that the person in trouble is sending the image, and is actually appearing to the recipient in some way. This suggests that the apparitions are a type of ghost.

The third view is that the apparitions are a manifestation of ESP. If this is the case, the receiver must be picking up a telepathic message from the person in distress, then somehow visualizing it.

 ## Figments of the imagination?

Crisis apparitions often appear to someone close to the person in trouble, so it may be anxiety about this person that creates a mental image of them. But this does not explain the McConnel case, as Larkin had no reason to worry about his friend. Also, this doesn't explain why the apparitions nearly always coincide with a major trauma.

Mrs. Collier's case offers another angle on this theory. She saw bandages around Joseph's head. Even if she had been worrying about him, it seems unlikely that she could have imagined the details of how he had been injured.

 ## A kind of ghost

The idea that the apparitions are a kind of ghost, sent by the person in trouble, does seem to fit Mrs. Collier's story. Joseph may have wanted her to know what had happened to him on the boat.

The ghost theory does not really explain Bonnie's experience, however, as Don did not appear in the room where she was; she saw a vision of the scene of his death.

Lieutenant Larkin's vision is also problematic. If Lieutenant McConnel sent an image of himself, why would he have made a mistake about his own death, saying that he had had "a good trip"?

 ## Telepathic vision

The ESP theory seems to work best for all three stories. Larkin may have had a strong feeling, or impression, about his friend without realizing that it signified his death.

Bonnie Mogyorossy could have had an experience of clairvoyance and "seen" what had happened to Don, visualizing the whole scene as well as the image of Don himself.

This theory even explains Mrs. Collier's vision of Joseph. If she could sense his death telepathically, it might also have been possible for her to pick up how it happened.

MODERN ESP TESTING

Scientists continue to carry out different kinds of tests for ESP, and to develop new techniques for doing so.

Restricted response testing

Some scientists are still using the techniques developed by Dr. Rhine[1], but they have refined them to make them more accurate. This sort of testing is called "restricted response" testing, because the subjects are tested on their ability to perceive specific targets such as Zener cards.

Free response testing

Other scientists use "free response" tests. This involves letting the mind run free and allowing images to form. The target in these experiments is something more complex than a simple shape, such as a scene or a short video clip.

[1]See page 49

Ganzfeld technique

In free response testing, it is thought that people perform best if their minds are free of distractions.

A popular way of achieving this is using the ganzfeld technique. The subject lies down comfortably under a red light. White noise (a gentle "ssshh" sound) is played through headphones to cut out other noises. Half table tennis balls are placed over the subject's eyes, to create a soft pinky-red light.

A "sender" transmits a randomly chosen target image, and the subject is asked to describe what comes to mind. This is then compared with the target image.

Success or failure?

The overall average for test results is just above what might be expected by chance. Therefore, many experimenters think that ESP may well exist, but if it does, it is very weak and unreliable.

A researcher assessing results

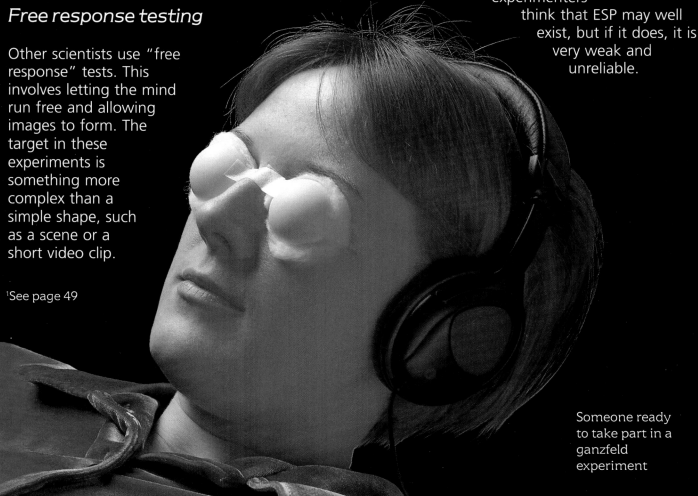

Someone ready to take part in a ganzfeld experiment

CHAPTER THREE: GHOSTS?

GHOSTLY ACTIVITY

Some people believe that ghosts are merely figments of our imaginations. Others believe that they are visions, or apparitions, of the dead. Some sightings, however, have been of people who are still alive; and there are also accounts of ghostly animals or even objects such as ships. Reports of ghostly activity have often included non-visual experiences such as noises, smells or sensations of coldness.

Where ghosts appear

Ghosts are often linked to particular locations. So, whereas poltergeists seem to focus on people, ghosts seem to attach themselves to places. Upon investigation, it sometimes turns out that significant events have occurred at these locations, and that some of the events were violent or traumatic in nature.

Ghost history

The case studies in this chapter range from accounts of historical hauntings to more modern ghostly sightings.

The earliest ghost reports are from over 2000 years ago. One early sighting was recorded by Pliny, a Roman writer. He told how in the 2nd century AD, a terrifying figure in chains appeared to Athenodorus, a Greek philosopher. The figure beckoned to Athenodorus, as if it wanted him to follow it. He did, but as they went out into the garden, the figure disappeared mysteriously.

The next day, Athenodorus had the garden dug up where the figure had disappeared. A skeleton bound in chains was found buried in the ground. It seemed as though the ghost was the spirit of this person, wandering around in order to draw attention to his remains.

Since the time of Pliny, accounts of ghosts have often followed a similar pattern. For many, as in this story, a possible explanation has been found, but no one can be sure that it is the right one.

This picture shows two 16th-century magicians, known as conjurors, calling up a spirit from the dead.

Case study 11: A ROMAN INVASION

Date: 1953 and 1957
Place: The Treasurer's House, York, England
Witnesses: Harry Martindale and Joan Mawson

THE EVENTS

Harry Martindale was installing central heating in the cellar of the Treasurer's House in York, when all of a sudden he heard an eerie noise. It seemed to be coming from deep within the walls. He put down his tools, and listened carefully. He decided it must be the sound of a radio in the building above.

An eerie noise

The sound grew steadily louder. Then, suddenly, a helmet bulged out of the wall. Harry stepped back in horror, tumbling from the ladder he was standing on. He scuttled into the corner of the cellar and watched in astonishment as a figure wearing a strange uniform and blowing a trumpet emerged. Behind him came a huge carthorse, followed by more figures who looked like soldiers.

The cellar where Harry was working

Figures wearing strange uniforms appeared from the wall of the cellar where Harry Martindale was working.

Missing legs

As the sound of the trumpet echoed around the cellar, Harry realized that it was the noise he had heard a few seconds before. He crouched down to observe the unexpected intruders.

Soldier after soldier trudged by. As they did, Harry noticed that, from the knees down, their legs disappeared into the floor. But when they crossed a section of the cellar where there was a hole in the floor, Harry caught a brief glimpse of their feet.

Military dress

The soldiers didn't pay any attention to Harry, so he had plenty of time to get a good look at them.

They were armed with round shields, spears, short swords and daggers. They dragged their feet heavily along the ground, seeming tired, as if returning from a battle or a long march.

The soldiers' bodies looked solid, though Harry knew in his heart that they were far from being real.

The last trumpet

Harry watched the trumpeter at the head of the procession cross the cellar and melt into the opposite wall. He was closely followed by the other soldiers. The sound of the trumpet lingered in the room even though the trumpeter could no longer be seen. It was only as the last soldier disappeared that the sound finally ceased.

Other reports

As soon as he was alone again, Harry wasted no time in rushing upstairs, where he met the curator who looked after a museum in the Treasurer's House. Seeing Harry's agitation, the curator guessed immediately what must have happened to him.

"By the look of you, you've seen the Romans, haven't you?" he said.

Harry was taken aback at this remark, but the curator seemed sympathetic, so at his suggestion, Harry wrote down everything he could remember about the incident.

When Harry had finished, the curator showed him two similar reports written by visitors who claimed to have seen the Romans. Harry was shocked, but relieved to discover that he was not the only person to have had such peculiar experiences.

The remains of a Roman sword and dagger, like the ones Harry saw the soldiers carrying

This picture shows the front of the Treasurer's House, York. It was in the cellar of this building that Roman soldiers were seen.

Case study 11: A ROMAN INVASION

A Roman road

In 1954, the year after Harry saw the Romans, archaeologist Peter Wenham began to excavate Roman remains beneath the Treasurer's House. He discovered what he believed to be the remains of a Roman road called the Via Decumana a little way below the modern floor of the cellar.

Part of the road had accidentally been exposed during earlier renovations to the house in around 1900, so even before Peter Wenham's excavations there was a hole in the floor of the cellar where the road had been uncovered. Significantly, it was when the soldiers crossed this hole that Harry was able to see their feet. As they crossed other areas of the floor, their feet disappeared. It was as if Harry was seeing the soldiers walking along the old Roman road.

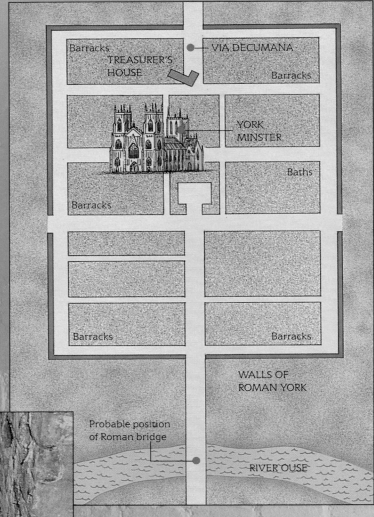

This map shows the position of the Roman roads around the Treasurer's House.

This Roman column base was exposed during renovations to the Treasurer's House in around 1900.

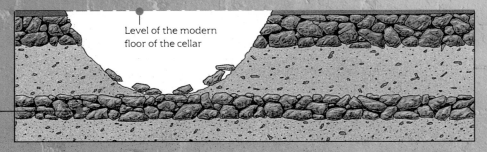

This diagram shows the hole in the cellar floor where Harry saw the Romans' feet.

The wrong shields

Initially, the fact that Harry described the Romans' shields as round cast doubt on his claims. The Roman foot soldiers, known as legionaries, in York would have been expected to use rectangular shields. It seemed as though his description was not historically accurate. In fact, Harry's descriptions turned out to be surprisingly accurate. In the 2nd century, when the surface of the Via Decumana exposed in the cellar dates from, the Roman army was made up of legionaries and soldiers called auxiliaries. The auxiliaries used round shields.

A rectangular shield like the ones carried by Roman foot soldiers

A round shield like the ones used by auxiliary soldiers in Roman armies

Going public

For some reason, Harry's story was not made public until 1974, over 20 years after his experience. It was only then that Joan Mawson, a caretaker at the Treasurer's House during the 1950s, told people about her own contact with Romans in the cellar.

The sound of hooves

It was on a Sunday evening in 1957 that Joan first saw the Romans. She went to the cellar of the Treasurer's House to check on the boiler. At first, her dog, a white bull terrier, ambled ahead of her. Then, suddenly, the dog ran howling from the cellar.

As Joan entered a narrow tunnel that led into the cellar, she thought she heard the sound of horses' hooves. A moment later she became aware of someone, or something, behind her. She turned and froze in terror. A group of Roman soldiers on horseback towered above her. She flattened herself against the wall, terrified that they would trample her underfoot, but the soldiers didn't seem to notice her.

Case study 11: A ROMAN INVASION

Weary troops

Joan Mawson saw the soldiers on two other occasions when she was alone in the cellar. The second time she saw them, they were splattered with mud and looked very tired.

On the third occasion, the soldiers looked extremely dishevelled and were slumped wearily over their horses' necks.

Many years passed before Joan told anyone about what she had seen.

A mystery guest

There is at least one other story relating to Romans seen at the Treasurer's House. It dates from the 1920s and has been passed down by word of mouth.

During a party given by a man named Frank Green, who owned the house at that time, a female guest went to the cellar, perhaps during a game of hide-and-seek. She found her way barred by someone dressed as a Roman soldier. Feeling puzzled, she returned to the party.

Many of the guests at the party were wearing costumes, but there was something odd about the incident. She mentioned it to the host, but Frank was insistent that there was nobody at the party who was dressed in a soldier's costume. Could it have been one of the ghostly Romans?

Someone dressed as a Roman soldier raised his hand to block the guest's way.

The details of Harry Martindale's story are very intricate and he appears to have the support of other witnesses. But did he really see ghosts, or are other explanations more likely?

Historical detail

If Harry was aware of the Roman history of the area surrounding the Treasurer's House or of the ghostly stories connected with the house itself, it's possible that he allowed his imagination to run wild.

However some elements of Harry's story seem quite convincing. For example, he couldn't have known about the round shields without a great deal of historical research. Yet Harry claims that

Harry Martindale, many years after his experience

before his ghostly experience he had no idea what Roman soldiers might have looked like. He had seen them in films, but said that they looked very different from the ones he had seen in the cellar.

If Harry did make up the story, it could be coincidence that his account happened to fit in with historical facts. York has a wealth of Roman history, so any research could quickly seem to suggest a match between a ghostly experience and earlier historical events or remains.

Unreliable memories

Joan Mawson's account adds weight to Harry's, but the delay before each of them made their stories public makes them less believable. Over time, people's memories can change and new details can be added. Also, the fact that Joan didn't tell anyone at the time makes it impossible to check her story.

Prompting

If the curator discussed the other ghostly reports with Harry before asking him to write down his story, Harry may have mixed up his own memories with events described by the curator. This kind of confusion could account for the similarities between the stories.

In this production of *The Romans in Britain*, the soldiers have rectangular shields. Harry's idea of what Romans looked like came from popular images such as this.

Case study 12: ECHOES OF BATTLE

Date: 1642 – 1643
Place: Edgehill and
Kineton, England
Witnesses: Multiple
witnesses

THE EVENTS

The dull, regular thud of drums began to draw closer. It was accompanied by agonized groans, as if people were crying out in pain and terror. Steadily, the noise became louder until it grew to a deafening roar.

Battle cries

In the middle of the field, a group of shepherds stood trembling with fear. Terrifying noises echoed all around, though the shepherds could see nothing. They started to run, but the noise still seemed to surround them. Then, suddenly, they were stopped dead in their tracks by an incredible sight.

In the air above, a terrible battle was raging. Hundreds of soldiers on horseback were riding furiously against one another, thrusting and slashing with their swords. Cannons belched forth clouds of thick, black smoke and muskets fired out deadly shots.

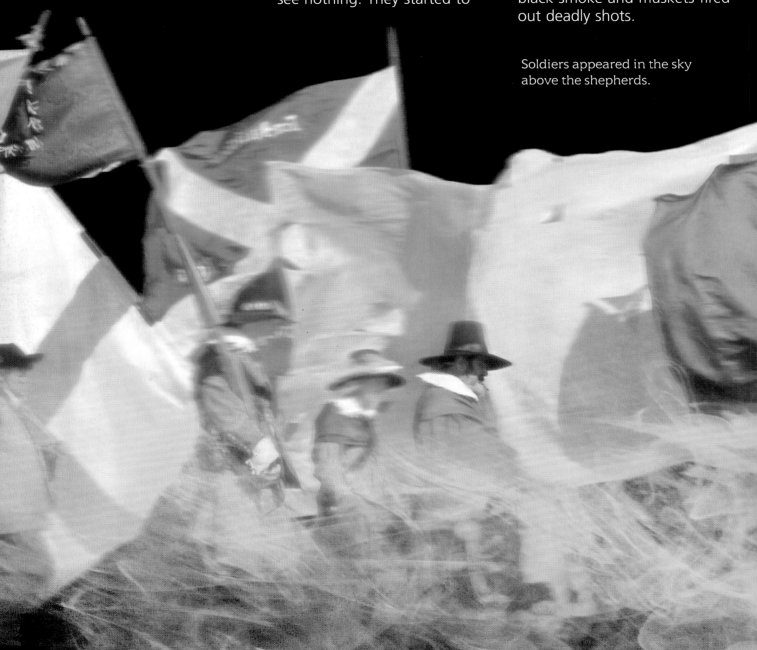

Soldiers appeared in the sky above the shepherds.

Clashing armies

The shepherds crouched down in the grass, barely moving in case the soldiers attacked them. Only a few moments before, they had been quietly tending their sheep in that very field. Now, suddenly, they were witnesses to an extraordinary vision.

Through the smoke, the shepherds could see people carrying flags which they recognized. The first battle of the English Civil War, known as the Battle of Edgehill, had been fought on that spot in October 1642, only a few months before. Had the troops from this battle somehow returned to fight again?

The shepherds' traumatic ordeal lasted several hours. Then the armies vanished as abruptly as they had appeared.

A strange story

As soon as the armies disappeared, the men hurried to the nearby town of Kineton and woke up Mr. Wood and Mr. Marshall, two respected members of the community, to tell them what had happened.

When Mr. Wood heard the story, he thought that the men must be drunk or crazy. But he had known some of the men for a long time and, sensing their genuine fear, felt he ought to take them seriously.

A second sighting

The next night, the shepherds took a group of people from Kineton to the place where they had seen the vision. After half an hour of waiting, the eerie battle began again. It was as violent and terrifying as the previous night.

The crashing of swords and pikes rang out as the soldiers locked together in deadly battle.

Disappearing horsemen

After these sightings, the armies were not seen for several nights, but then a group of strangers to the town reported meeting soldiers of a similar description on the road.

They said that a troop of horsemen had ridden past them and then sunk mysteriously into the ground. When the newcomers told their tale, the townspeople mocked them. But they were quickly forced to change their attitudes.

A town in terror

On January 4th, in the middle of the night, the people of Kineton woke up trembling as the battle began again. Some hid in corners, while others lay sweating under their covers. Only a few brave individuals peered out of their windows. They saw horsemen racing along the road.

Driven away

The next night, a small group gathered to stand guard at the town's gates. At midnight, the soldiers appeared again. For many people the experience was too much. The next day, they gathered up a few belongings and left Kineton.

Kineton is about 3km (2 miles) from the Edgehill battlefield.

Informing the king

Mr. Marshall decided to take charge of the situation. He went to Oxford to inform King Charles. Intrigued by the story, the king sent some men to Edgehill to investigate.

An engraving of the ghostly battle from a 17th-century pamphlet that decribed the strange events

A bust of King Charles I, whose troops fought at Edgehill

Familiar faces

The king's men were amazed at the sight that met them the following Saturday when the vision appeared just as before.

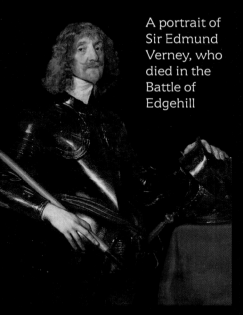

A portrait of Sir Edmund Verney, who died in the Battle of Edgehill

As they watched the battling armies, they recognized the flags and uniforms of their own troops and even the faces of some of the soldiers.

They then realized with horror that several of the soldiers, including their friend Sir Edmund Verney, were men who had fought and died at the Battle of Edgehill several months previously.

A peaceful end

The phantoms continued to appear, to the distress of the residents of Kineton. Finally, someone suggested that the apparitions might be the restless souls of the dead. A search of the battlefield revealed a number of unburied bodies. Shortly after, when the bodies had been buried, the visions finally ceased.

The site of the Battle of Edgehill today

The English Civil War

In the 1640s, England was divided by a struggle for power between King Charles I and Parliament. This led to the outbreak of civil war in 1642.

The first major conflict of the Civil War took place at Edgehill in October 1642. Neither side had a clear victory and many soldiers were killed.

Many of those who witnessed the mysterious apparitions at Edgehill believed that what they had seen may have been some sort of ghostly reenactment or replay of that battle.

Oliver Cromwell, pictured at the front of this group of horsemen, was the leader of the Parliamentarians. This painting by Ernest Crofts shows his troops after a Civil War battle known as the Battle of Marston Moor.

Reports of such vivid and lengthy apparitions, and ones with so many witnesses are rare. Yet it is difficult to confirm the facts of a case that happened so long ago.

Superstitious times

In the 17th century, belief in the supernatural was more widespread than it is today. Across Europe, many hundreds of people were drowned or burned as witches. Belief in fairies and magic was commonplace, and ghosts were often reported.

Ghosts also appeared in the literature of the era, featuring in two of Shakespeare's most famous plays, *Macbeth* and *Hamlet*. Perhaps the story of the Edgehill ghosts was invented by people caught up in the superstitious atmosphere of the time.

Political pamphlets

The ghostly Battle of Edgehill was described in two pamphlets written in the 17th century. However, these pamphlets are not necessarily reliable accounts of what

actually happened. At that time, pamphlets were sometimes produced for political reasons to try to influence people's opinions. The pamphlets about the battle are openly political, calling for an end to the Civil War, and for God to bring King Charles to his senses.

A 17th-century pamphlet which describes the ghostly battle

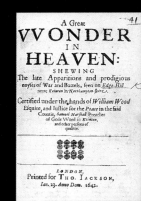

A Great
VVONDER
IN
HEAVEN:
SHEWING
The late Apparitions and prodigious noyses of War and Battels, seen on *Edge-Hill* neere *Keinton* in *Northampton* shire.

Certified under the hands of *William Wood* Esquire, and Iustice for the *Peace* in the said Countie, *Samuel Marshall* Preacher of Gods Word in *Keinton*, and other persons of qualitie.

LONDON,
Printed for THO. IACKSON,
Ian. 23. *Anno Dom.* 1642.

A scene from a modern performance of Shakespeare's play *Macbeth*, which features three witches

ACTION REPLAYS

Some paranormal investigators have suggested that certain apparitions may be recordings of events from a previous era. They believe that they are like video or sound recordings, but that what is played back is a scene, sounds or sensations from the past.

Frozen in time

The term "recording ghosts" is given to apparitions that always appear in the same place. They seem unaware of the people who witness them and of their modern surroundings. It's as if the ghosts are fixed in a particular time and space.

One explanation that has been offered for ghosts walking through walls is that this type of ghost moves around a building as it was in its own time. People have suggested that when a ghost walks through a wall it is because there used to be a door there.

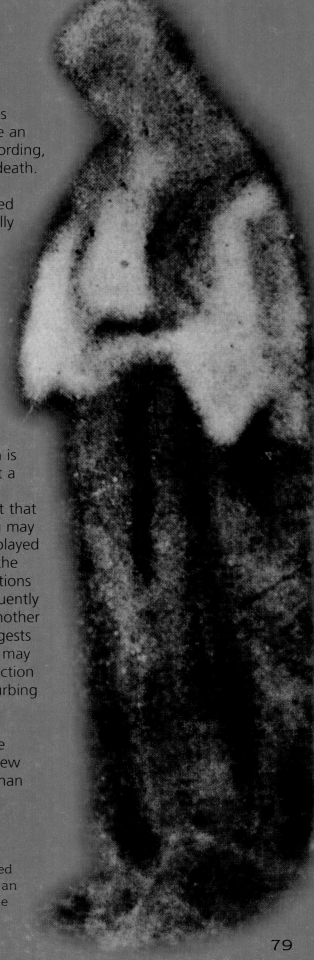

Could minerals such as quartz be capable of storing information?

How are recordings made?

When we are afraid or stressed, we produce a high level of emotional energy. One theory offered to explain recording ghosts suggests that under certain conditions this energy is stored at a particular location. So, if someone is distressed, they may leave an emotional imprint, or recording, which lingers after their death.

No clear scientific argument has been offered to explain how this actually happens. It has been suggested that the presence of a particular mineral in the walls or surroundings may be relevant. For example, the mineral quartz produces an electric field when pressure is applied to it. Perhaps this somehow enables it to store information, which is then released at a later date.

It is thought that a recording may then be replayed whenever the right conditions are subsequently created. Another theory suggests that replay may be triggered by reconstruction or excavation works disturbing a building.

Without clear scientific evidence to support these theories, it's difficult to view them as anything more than speculation.

It is claimed that this photograph, taken in 1897, shows the spirit of a girl called Ninia. Could Ninia have left an energy behind her that made this impression on the film?

Case study 13: THE HAUNTED HOTEL

Date: June, 1969
Place: Wales (town's name is not recorded)
Witness: Detective Inspector D. Elvet Price

THE EVENTS

The night began with a strange incident, although at the time Inspector Price had thought little of it. He had come up from London early that morning to make inquiries about a case he was working on and was spending the night at a hotel in a small Welsh town.

Just before going to bed, he had gone out to the bathroom in the corridor outside his room. On his way, he met a woman dressed in long, old-fashioned clothes. He greeted her, but she didn't respond. She continued along the corridor as if in a trance.

The inspector assumed that the woman just hadn't heard him. It was only later events that made him wonder who or what she was.

A woman walked straight past the inspector, as if in a trance.

A rude awakening

It wasn't long before Inspector Price was sleeping soundly. Some time later, he woke up suddenly, his heart pounding. Choking and gasping noises were coming from the floor beside his bed. Only half-awake, he scrambled over to the light switch. As he did, a strange sensation of coldness enveloped him.

As soon as the inspector switched on the light, the noises and the sensation of coldness stopped. He looked all around, even under the bed, but the room was empty.

He glanced at his watch. It was 1:30am. He felt confused and unsettled. In case there had been an intruder in his room, he slipped his wallet and watch under the pillow and settled back down to sleep.

The inspector put his wallet and watch under the pillow for safety.

A disturbing night

Despite this odd experience, the inspector slept soundly. But before long, his sleep was interrupted by the sounds of a struggle for the second time that night. Again he switched on the light and again the noises stopped. It was 3:00am.

At 4:15am he was woken up for a third time. As he listened to the blood-curdling noises, the inspector felt a clammy coldness creep over him. Then, unable to bear the horrific sound of suffering, he switched on the light. The noises ceased immediately.

Each time the inspector switched on the light, the noises stopped.

Lights on

Inspector Price had had enough. Even a long career with the police had not prepared him for such strange happenings. This time he decided to keep the light on. Eventually, exhaustion overwhelmed him and he drifted off to sleep. To his relief, when he next woke up it was morning.

Case study 13: THE HAUNTED HOTEL

Keeping quiet

The next day, Inspector Price was met by Sergeant Jones, the local policeman who had booked the hotel for him. The inspector didn't mention his strange experiences for fear he would be ridiculed. Yet he couldn't stop thinking about what he had heard.

A week later, back in London, the inspector met another policeman from the Welsh town. He was so curious about what had happened that he told him the story, but swore the man to secrecy. The man then revealed that the hotel was reported to be haunted. The story behind the haunting was a violent one.

A violent death

According to local stories, in 1909 the hotel had been the scene of an horrific and violent death. Angharad Llewellyn, the wife of the landlord, had been brutally murdered. She had been beaten and strangled in her bedroom. Inspector Price realized with a feeling of sickness and horror that the sounds he had heard must have been a bizarre replay of the woman's dying moments.

The real story

He listened in shock as the policeman told him how the woman's husband had been found guilty of her murder and hanged.

In fact, when Inspector Price later researched the story himself, he discovered that the murder had taken place in 1920. He also found out that the husband had not been hanged but had received a five-year prison sentence. The judge had in fact concluded that the man had assaulted his wife, but had not intended to kill her.

The hotel landlord strangled his wife, though the judge later concluded that he had not intended to kill her.

Case study 13: THE ASSESSMENT

The documents from the murder trial seem likely to offer evidence to support this story. However, since the name of the town where it occurred has not been recorded, the details are difficult to confirm.

Silent lady

The inspector assumed that the woman he saw was the ghost of the murder victim. However, she could easily have been another guest or a member of the hotel staff.

Just a dream?

During his troubled night, every time Inspector Price switched on the light, the noises stopped. One possible explanation for this is that he may have been having a recurrent nightmare and it was only when he switched on the light that he woke up fully. Often when we first wake up from a dream, it still seems extremely vivid, while just a few moments later it may seem much less realistic.

Inaccurate story

Inspector Price's original interpretation of his experience as a haunting was based on local stories rather than known facts. When he investigated the story for himself, he found that details of the actual events had been distorted to produce a more dramatic and sinister tale. The connecting of the "ghost" with the murder story may similarly have been the result of gossip and speculation.

Sleepy visions

One explanation for what Inspector Price heard is that he was hallucinating. When falling asleep, people sometimes experience vivid sensations, called hypnogogic visions, which are a little like nightmares. Similar visions, known as hypnopompic visions, can occur when waking up.

These kinds of visions (or, in the inspector's case, sounds) can be very realistic and frightening. The sleeper often feels a sense of being trapped and sometimes experiences choking sensations. Perhaps the inspector mistook his own choking and gasping for that of someone else.

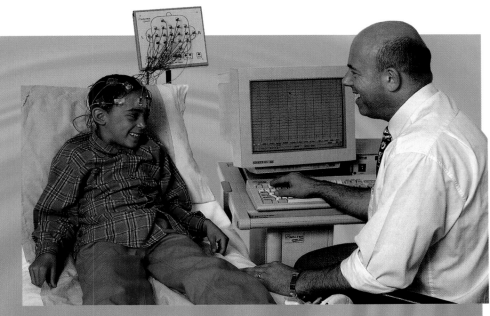

Scientists find out about people's experiences during sleep by monitoring their brain activity using an electroencephalogram (EEG) like this one.

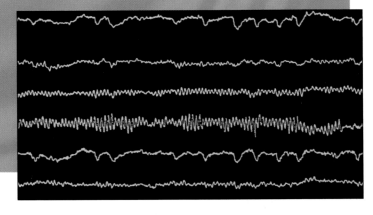

An EEG chart shows when the brain is most active.

PHOTOGRAPHING GHOSTS

Ghosts are notoriously difficult to capture on film. However, there are a few examples of photographs of ghosts. With modern cameras and computer programs, it is easy to fake ghost photographs; but for pictures taken many years ago techniques for faking were more limited.

Transparent images

Most people who claim to have seen ghosts describe them as solid-looking. Yet most photographs of ghosts show transparent figures like the one below, known as the Brown Lady.

The Brown Lady was photographed at Raynham Hall in 1936 by Captain Provand and Indre Shira. As the photograph was taken, Indre saw a figure, but the captain saw nothing. Perhaps Indre tampered with the photograph in order to convince him.

The ghostly Brown Lady of Raynham Hall

Great-grandmother pays a visit

In 1991, Greg Maxwell pointed up into the air as his photograph was taken and said "Old Nana's here". When the photograph (shown below) was developed, Greg's family recalled the remark that he had made and concluded that the white cloud in the photograph was the ghost of Greg's great-grandmother who had died a short time before.

Greg Maxwell and "Nana", 1991

The fuzzy shapeless white form on the left of the photograph could be almost anything – a reflection from a light or shiny object, or a finger over the camera lens. What makes it seem significant is Greg's comment and his attentive gaze.

A fiery girl

When developed, this photograph of a fire at Wem Town Hall, Shropshire, in 1995, revealed a young girl. People suggested she may have been the ghost of a young girl who had caused an earlier fire at Wem in 1677, when her candle set light to the thatched roof of the building.

Analysts have suggested that the figure may be an optical illusion caused by shadows of the flames and falling wood. Alternatively, it might be a double exposure, which means that two separate pictures have been combined on a single piece of film. Nevertheless, the final result makes a convincing ghost photograph.

A close-up of the mysterious girl at Wem Town Hall surrounded by flames

Tulip Staircase

When Reverend Hardy took a photograph of the Tulip Staircase in the National Maritime Museum in 1966, he couldn't see the eerie figures that appear on the picture.

At first glance, the figure at the bottom of the stairs looks like a hooded spirit. However, another explanation seems more likely. Reverend Hardy didn't use a flash. Instead he gave the picture a long exposure, keeping the camera's shutter open for several seconds to allow enough light in. If, during this time, someone had dashed upstairs, their image could have been captured several times in a single picture.

Left: Reverend Hardy's photograph of the Tulip Staircase ghosts. It is kept in the National Maritime Museum, Greenwich

The picture on the right, taken by Brian Tremain, shows how a person hurrying up the staircase would be captured on film.

Case study 14: THE HOUSE OF FACES

Date: From August 23rd, 1971
Place: Bélmez de la Moraleda, Spain
Witnesses: The Pereira family and other witnesses

THE EVENTS

On August 23rd, 1971, Maria Pereira caught sight of a mark on her kitchen floor. She scrubbed at it, but it didn't fade. Over the next few days, the mark became more clearly defined and started to bear an uncanny resemblance to a face. Gradually, it grew clearer until there was no longer any doubt. A face was staring up from the floor and no amount of scrubbing would remove it.

Destroying faces

Maria and her husband, Juan, a farmer and shepherd, were afraid. They couldn't understand what was happening in their house. Wanting to protect his parents, their son Miguel intervened, using a sledgehammer to destroy the part of the floor where the face was. But soon after, a second face began to form on another part of the floor.

The council intervenes

News of the mysterious faces soon spread around the quiet town of Bélmez. Eventually, the story came to the attention of the local council, which sent someone to cut out the part of the floor containing the faces. But tests conducted on it revealed nothing unusual.

Bélmez is a small town in southern Spain.

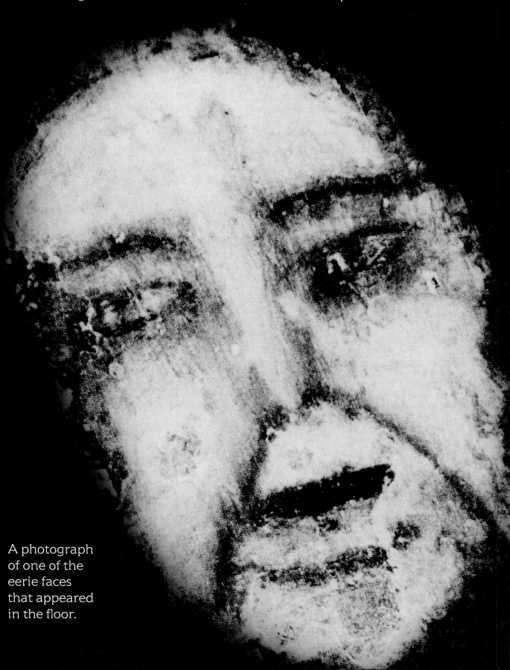

A photograph of one of the eerie faces that appeared in the floor.

For a few days it seemed as if the Pereiras had seen the last of the faces. Then, suddenly, another one appeared. Miguel destroyed it, but as soon as the floor was repaired yet another face formed. It was a woman's face, her hair flying as if caught by the wind. More faces appeared around her.

After a time, some of the faces faded and disappeared, but new ones appeared in their place. Sometimes small crosses appeared too.

Skeletons uncovered

The story generated a frenzy of interest. People came from miles around, hoping to get a glimpse of the faces. Some researchers became interested too. Among them was Professor de Argumosa, a lecturer at the University of Madrid. He discovered an intriguing story which might be connected with the faces.

In the 17th century, a cruel governor of the province of Granada had ordered the murders of five members of a local family. When part of the floor of the Pereiras' house was dug up, human remains were found buried below the floor. Among them were two headless skeletons.

Professor de Argumosa decided to conduct a simple experiment on the faces. He divided the floor into sections and took photographs of each section. He then covered the floor with foil and sealed it at the edges so that the faces could not be tampered with. When the foil was removed, he discovered that the faces had continued to change beneath it. Unless someone had removed the foil and then replaced it, the faces could not have been altered by human hands.

This face, which seems to be a woman's, appeared in late 1971.

These mysterious eyes appeared in the floor in June 1972.

Different faces

Many different kinds of faces appeared in the floor: one was a child's, another a beautiful woman's and a third a bald old man's. The expressions on the faces would sometimes change, or other details of their appearance would alter.

Parts of their bodies occasionally appeared too. One woman's hand was visible as well as her face. She was holding a flower. Gradually, over a period of time, the flower was transformed into a cup. Nobody knew what the significance of these changes might be.

This face became known as "the bald one".

Sudden changes

Not all the changes were gradual. On one occasion, Jos Martínez Romero, who later wrote a book about the case, saw faces appearing and disappearing at random. Othe witnessed the faces forming, not over a period of days, but before their very eyes.

Mr. Romero and author Andrew MacKenzie examining a face

Cries of the dead?

Most disturbing of all the events in the Pereiras' house were noises revealed on audio recordings made by Professor de Argumosa. No noises were heard in the room when the recordings were made, but when they were played back, terrifying cries and groans were heard mingling with murmuring voices.

Professor de Argumosa was even able to pick out a few words. He heard in Spanish what sounded like "spirits", "drunkard", "little grandchild", "Poor Cico" and "What will become of your life?". Whatever the story behind the voices, it seemed like a tragic one.

Case study 14: THE ASSESSMENT

The faces of Bélmez have continued to appear for over 20 years and have been examined by numerous witnesses. Yet experts still can't agree about what they are.

Works of art

People have said that the faces look like paintings. After a chemical analysis of the faces, an inquiry led by parapsychologist J.L. Jordán concluded that this was exactly what they were. He suggested that they may have been created using soot and vinegar or cleaning chemicals. Yet there were other scientists who conducted tests, but found no evidence of unusual chemicals.

If the faces are paintings, this does not explain how they formed before people's eyes.

Spirits of the dead

The story of the murders and the discovery of the skeletons led to suggestions that the faces were caused by the unsettled spirits of the dead. Unfortunately, because the story dates from the 17th century, none of the faces could be identified as any of the murder victims, so it has been impossible to establish any definite connection.

Psychokinesis?

The faces seemed to be connected with Maria. She was the first to see them and they were said to be darker when she was in poor health. People wondered whether she had created the faces using her mind. This ability to influence objects mentally is known as psychokinesis. There are people who claim to have such abilities. In the 1960s, a man named Ted Serios claimed he could visualize an image, such as a building, and photograph his thought.

In the case of the Pereira family, deliberate fraud cannot be ruled out, although there is no clear evidence as to how they went about it.

A thought photograph of the Capitol building, Washington, USA taken by Ted Serios

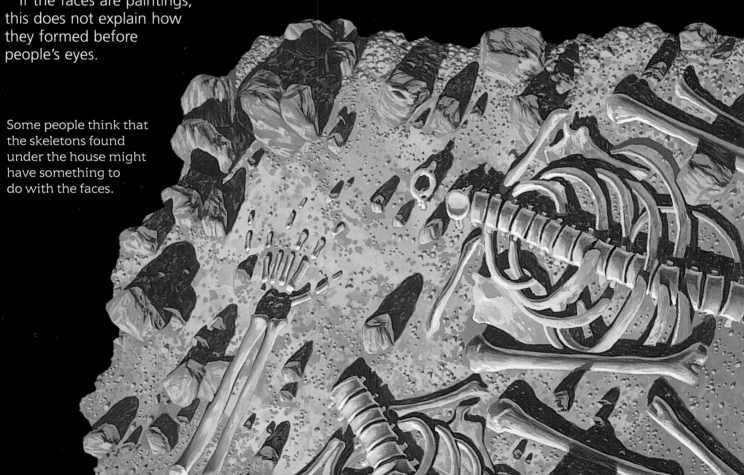

Some people think that the skeletons found under the house might have something to do with the faces.

Case study 15: A DEADLY DISASTER

Date: 1972 – 1973
Place: Eastern Airlines'
L-1011 airliners
Witnesses: Multiple
witnesses

THE EVENTS

It was a moonless night in the Everglades National Park, Florida, USA. Former wildlife officer Bob Marquis was looking for frogs. As he skimmed across the expanse of reeds and water in his airboat, he noticed an airliner flying low in the sky.

Moments later, a bright orange flash cut across the night sky. Then darkness returned to the Everglades. The airliner Bob had just seen had disappeared from the sky. At the same time, in the flight control room at Miami airport, Charles Johnson noticed that flight 401 was no longer appearing on the radar system. The full horror of the situation soon became clear to him. The plane had plummeted into a remote part of the Everglades.

The flight paths of aircraft are tracked using a radar system like this one.

Crash horror

Meanwhile, in the Everglades, Bob Marquis guessed that the plane had crashed. He realized that he might be the only person for miles around, and felt suddenly lonely in the wilderness. With only a small lamp tied around his head to guide him, he turned his tiny airboat and set off in the direction of the crash.

Bob Marquis saw an airliner flying low over the Everglades.

Guiding light

The sound of hysterical screams and cries of agony guided Bob to the site of the crash. As he moved his head, the flickering beam of his lamp picked out the pale, frightened faces of the living, and the limp bodies of the dead.

Bob felt desperately alone. The icy water was shallow, but it seemed ominous as it washed over the survivors trapped in the wreckage. He tried to help people, but the tall grass and the weight of the water held him back as he waded among the jagged remains of the aircraft. It seemed an eternity before help came.

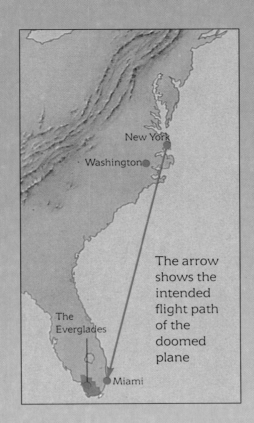

The arrow shows the intended flight path of the doomed plane

An inquiry

Of the 176 people on board flight 401 on December 29th, 1972, only 75 survived.

In the weeks after the crash, the National Transportation Safety Board began to piece together what had happened that night. At first, the cause of the crash was a mystery. The crew had been having minor technical problems, but seemed to have them under control. The flight controller's only clue that something was wrong was a radar reading from shortly before the crash which showed that the plane was flying unusually low. That was the last record of the flight before it hit the ground.

The debris from Flight 401 had been hurled in all directions.

Rescue workers used airboats to reach the survivors of the plane crash.

Case study 15: A DEADLY DISASTER

Who was to blame?

Gradually, a fuller picture of what had happened emerged. The inquiry into the disaster concluded that the crew had been distracted by technical problems shortly before the crash. However, other problems with the information on their displays may also have contributed to the disaster.

The most significant revelation was that a safety device that allowed the pilot to override the plane's automatic pilot system in an emergency had been badly designed. This meant that the automatic pilot could be disengaged accidentally by someone leaning across the controls.

The final moments

The co-pilot's computer and the captain's had different settings. This may have meant that the co-pilot's display did not show a change in altitude when the automatic pilot disengaged. The captain's controls did show this information, but the captain didn't notice it.

It was only in the final few seconds before the crash that the co-pilot realized that something was wrong. "We did something to the altitude," he said. Then a moment later he called out, "Hey, what's happening here?" But it was too late.

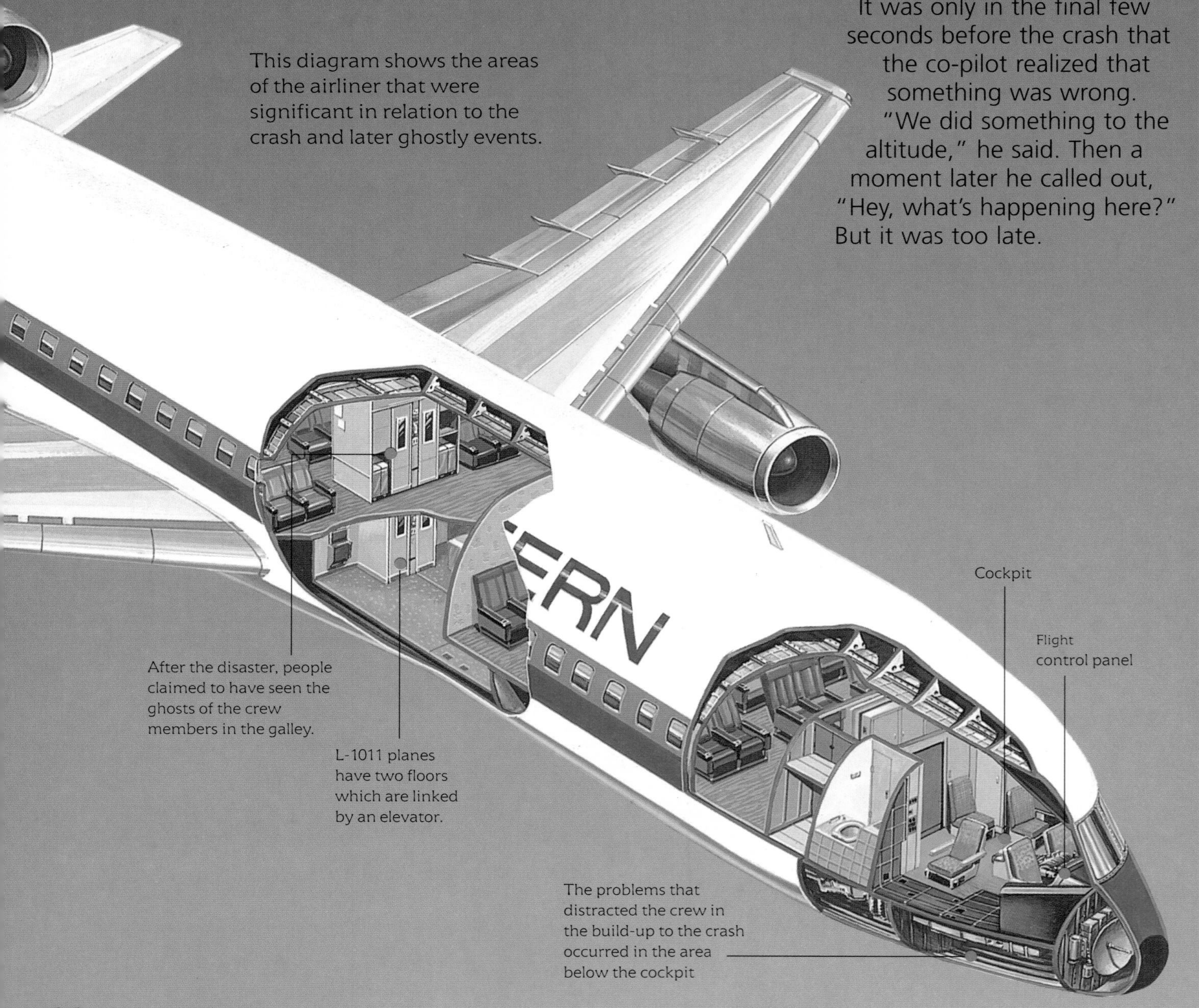

This diagram shows the areas of the airliner that were significant in relation to the crash and later ghostly events.

After the disaster, people claimed to have seen the ghosts of the crew members in the galley.

L-1011 planes have two floors which are linked by an elevator.

The problems that distracted the crew in the build-up to the crash occurred in the area below the cockpit

Cockpit

Flight control panel

A disappearing passenger

In the weeks after the accident, some unusual stories began to circulate. On a number of L-1011 planes (the same kind of plane as the one that had crashed), people claimed to have seen the ghosts of the crew members who had died on flight 401. A passenger on one flight sat beside a man who was wearing a flight engineer's uniform. He looked pale, so she asked how he was. He didn't respond.

Don Repo was the engineer on flight 401.

The woman called the stewardess over. But when she came, the man disappeared. The passenger became hysterical and began to scream. Nothing the stewardess said could console her. She demanded to see photographs of all Eastern Airways' flight engineers. From these, she was able to identify the man she had seen. It was Don Repo, the engineer who died on flight 401.

A strange mist

On another flight, a stewardess was in the galley waiting for the elevator when she caught sight of a hazy cloud nearby. It seemed to be pulsating. She stabbed urgently at the elevator button. She had heard some of the stories and had no desire to remain there on her own.

As she waited, she tried not to look at the shape. But, out of the corner of her eye, she saw it form into a face.

She could even see a pair of steel-rimmed glasses appearing. Eventually, the elevator came and she made her escape.

As the stewardess stood by the elevator, the mysterious cloud formed into a face.

Case study 15: A DEADLY DISASTER

Captain Loft's face
was staring down from
an overhead locker.

Face to face

Some Eastern Airlines' staff
who had known Captain Loft
and Don Repo personally
reported seeing their ghosts.
One flight attendant opened an
overhead locker to find Captain
Loft's face staring at her.

On another occasion, a
captain and two flight
attendants spotted Captain
Loft sitting in the first class
section of a plane.

In a sighting on another
flight, a senior Eastern Airlines'
representative started to talk to
someone he thought was the
flight's captain. He had been
speaking for some time before
he realized that he was talking
to Bob Loft.

A ghostly protector

The ghost of engineer Don
Repo seemed to want to
watch over other flights. He
said to one captain, "There
will never be another crash of
an L-1011. . . we will not let
it happen."

Another time, he told an
engineer about to conduct a
preflight check, "You don't
need to worry about the
preflight. I've already done it."

Near disaster

On another flight, crew
members saw the face of Don
Repo appear in an oven door.
It gave a warning that was to
prove uncannily close to the
mark: "Watch out for fire on
this plane."

On the next part of their
journey, the crew had problems
with two of the three engines
and had to land the plane
using the one remaining
engine. They brought it down
safely, but could this have been
because Don Repo was looking
after them?

Case study 15: THE ASSESSMENT

A dusty old mansion seems a more typical location for a haunting than a large airliner, yet people frequently claim to have seen apparitions in such modern environments.

Anonymous witnesses

During the research for his book, *The Ghost of Flight 401*, John Fuller interviewed many people who claimed to have seen the ghostly crew members. Most of the witnesses were people who worked on other flights.

It is claimed that Eastern Airlines put pressure on their employees not to talk about their encounters. As a result, most witnesses preferred to remain anonymous. Unfortunately this makes it difficult to check their accounts.

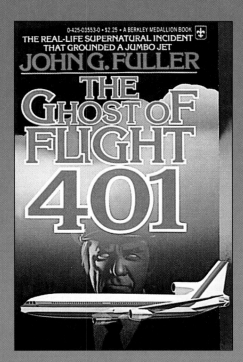

THE REAL-LIFE SUPERNATURAL INCIDENT THAT GROUNDED A JUMBO JET
0-425-03553-0 • $2.25 • A BERKLEY MEDALLION BOOK

JOHN G. FULLER

THE GHOST OF FLIGHT 401

John Fuller's book, *The Ghost of Flight 401*

Kim Basinger and Ernest Borgnine in the movie *The Ghost of Flight 401*

Expecting a ghost

The ghostly sightings all took place on L-1011 airliners, the same model as the one that crashed. Following the crash, passengers and crew members on these Eastern Airlines flights were probably feeling anxious and preoccupied with the disaster, worried that the same thing could happen to them. Crew members may also have been suffering from grief, after the deaths of their colleagues.

The combination of these factors, together with the stories about ghosts being circulated, may have prepared people's imaginations for ghostly occurrences, causing them to hallucinate or to misinterpret shadows in poor lighting as faces.

Missing log books

Some of the ghostly sightings were supposedly recorded by crew members in flight log books, where anything that happens on the flight is noted down. Unfortunately, these log books disappeared mysteriously. It is claimed that senior Eastern Airlines' staff often asked for log books to be replaced before previous log books were full. Were the witnesses' reports being hushed up, or was the story merely an excuse for the absence of this important evidence?

CHAPTER FOUR:
ALIENS?

CLOSE ENCOUNTERS

A recent survey in America revealed that 26 per cent of Americans believe that they have seen an Unidentified Flying Object (UFO). That is 90 million people. There have also been thousands of sightings in other places around the world, and many people claim to have been actually abducted by aliens. So can you really be sure it won't happen to you?

Fact or fiction?

Many of the thousands of close encounters reported each year are studied by enthusiasts called UFOlogists. They spend their time searching for evidence of Extra Terrestrial life, which means life beyond our planet, and for signs that alien beings really are here among us.

Most sightings turn out to be misidentifications. What people think are UFOs often turn out to be nothing more than an aircraft, a weather balloon, the moon, a flock of birds or even a swarm of insects.

To this day, however, over 200,000 sightings remain a complete mystery, and the witnesses involved remain convinced that they have encountered aliens. Some people think that the kind of person who sees a UFO has an over-active imagination; but it seems incredible that so many people could be mistaken.

The beginning

The study of UFOs and aliens really started in 1947, when a man named Kenneth Arnold was flying a plane over the Cascade mountains in Washington State, USA. He saw nine unidentified objects, flying at great speed. When the press heard his story, they described the objects as flying saucers. The idea of aliens visiting our planet began to be taken seriously. Governments spent money investigating reports and attempting to contact alien life-forms.

Don't panic!

It is very hard to prove conclusively whether aliens really are visiting our planet. In the end, it is up to you to read the case studies and decide what you believe.

If, when you have read the accounts in this chapter, you feel that there is strong evidence to suggest that aliens do actually exist – don't panic! If they are here, they have probably been visiting our planet for several centuries, and they haven't harmed us yet.

Are aliens visiting Earth in spacecraft that can travel faster than the speed of light?

Case study 16: MANTELL'S FATAL FLIGHT

Date: January 7th, 1948
Time: 1:35pm
Place: Godman Airfield near Fort Knox, Kentucky, USA
Witness: Captain Thomas Mantell Jr.

THE EVENTS

The Chief of Police wanted to know what on earth was going on. All morning his office had been inundated with reports of a mysterious UFO. The people of Maysville, Kentucky, had jammed his telephone lines with tales of a huge, round object floating silently through the sky.

When quizzed, most of them described something that was shaped like a parachute, over 75m (250 ft) wide, and looked like it was made of metal. Even a highway patrolman had radioed in to report seeing a vast silver shape overhead.

Looking for answers

At 1:15pm, the Chief of Police picked up the phone and called the nearby airbase at Godman. Could the US Air Force give him any information about the strange phenomenon that was alarming the townspeople?

His inquiry was relayed to the Air Force Test Center at Wright-Patterson Airfield. But the Air Force insisted that no aircraft fitting that description was being tested in the area. People must simply be imagining things.

On the radar

Imaginary or not, at 1:35pm radar scanners in the Godman Flight Control Tower picked up an unidentified craft approaching from the southeast at a height of 3,950m (13,000ft). Minutes later, airmen down on the runway spotted something too.

A Flight Control Tower radar operator of the time

UFO sighted

It was clearly no ordinary aircraft. Even though they scrutinized it through binoculars, the men couldn't identify it. The object hovered motionless above the airfield for a full half hour, glowing with an eerie red light. Then it shot up into the clouds before stopping again.

Mustangs investigate

Suddenly, over the radio at the Godman Tower, came the voice of 25-year-old Captain Thomas Mantell. He was leading a flight of four P-51 Mustang fighters. Reporting their position as 16km (10 miles) south of Godman, Mantell asked the Tower's permission to fly over the airfield.

The Tower radioed back: the Mustangs were to alter their course and check out the UFO. With his excitement obvious in his voice, Captain Mantell acknowledged the new instructions and immediately changed his course. The chase was on.

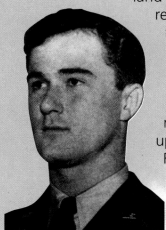

Captain Thomas Mantell

A deadly pursuit

One of the Mustangs was low on fuel and its pilot decided to land immediately. The remaining three began to climb, attempting to intercept the mysterious craft.

At 6,700m (22,000ft) Captain Mantell's two remaining pilots gave up the chase. US Air Force regulations demanded that oxygen supplies must be used by any pilots flying over an altitude of 4,200m (14,000ft). This was in order to prevent pilots experiencing breathing difficulties due to the lack of oxygen in the air at that altitude. However, none of the P-51 Mustangs was equipped with oxygen.

Before they broke off pursuit, the two pilots radioed Captain Mantell, trying to warn him that he was flying dangerously high without oxygen, but he flew on, climbing to 7,000m (23,000ft).

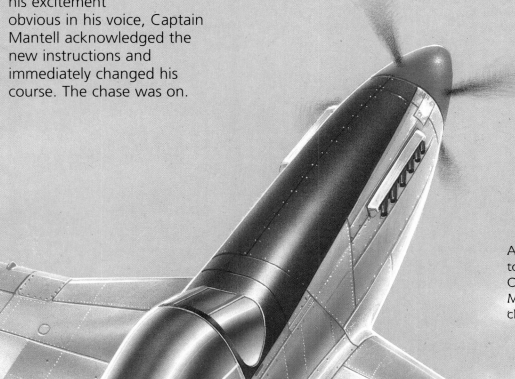

As two pilots turned back toward the airbase, Captain Mantell's P-51 Mustang continued to climb toward the UFO.

Case study 16: MANTELL'S FATAL FLIGHT

Newspaper report

Several newspapers later reported that Captain Mantell had radioed Godman Tower with the following words: "It's fantastic! It's right above me, and it's tremendous! It looks metallic, and it's huge and circular. It could be anything between 500 and 1,000 feet across. It seems to be cruising at about 200 knots, and I'm gaining on it. It's colossal! I'm going to try and get above it. It's climbing! It's starting to climb... God, this is fantastic! It's getting hot. It's hot! The heat! I can't..."

This account is typical of how UFO stories can be exaggerated and sensationalized in newspaper reports. All that Captain Mantell actually said before his radio went dead was that he had spotted the UFO above him, that it was large and metallic, and he was gaining on it.

A terrible end

These were the last words Captain Mantell ever transmitted. He was found two hours later. A search party came across his Mustang crashed into a field outside Franklin, Kentucky. It had exploded on impact. Inside the cockpit, they found Captain Mantell's body. His watch had stopped at 3:18pm. The search team decided that this must have been the time of the crash.

Captain Mantell's body was found inside the cockpit of his P-51 Mustang.

Official statement

Almost immediately, stories began to circulate about the crash. Most people believed that Captain Mantell's plane had been shot down by the UFO. In the end, the US Air Force issued a statement: Captain Mantell's P-51 Mustang had broken up in midair as a result of flying too high. They claimed that Captain Mantell had been chasing the planet Venus, which had appeared strangely magnified in the sky because of rare weather conditions.

A change of story

Realizing that nobody believed this explanation, the Air Force released another statement. This time they claimed that Mantell had died while chasing a weather balloon. For over 30 years this remained the official explanation of the fatal flight.

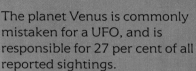

The planet Venus is commonly mistaken for a UFO, and is responsible for 27 per cent of all reported sightings.

Case study 16: THE ASSESSMENT

Many strange and exaggerated stories grew up around Captain Thomas Mantell's death. Some were prompted by the Air Force releasing misleading statements; others were caused by sensational newspaper reports.

Chasing Venus

The US Air Force's original statement that Captain Mantell had been chasing the planet Venus was an unlikely explanation. On a sunny afternoon it would have been very difficult to see the planet. In addition, Venus wouldn't have been picked up by the radar at Godman Tower, nor would it have been described by witnesses as a large, shiny metal object moving close to the Earth.

Listening devices

In 1985, the Air Force changed their story again. They admitted that Captain Mantell was chasing a Skyhook balloon. The balloons had been secretly released by the US Navy from Camp Ripley in Minnesota, and were floating over the area.

They were huge, 135m (450ft) tall and 30m (100ft) across, and matched the descriptions given by witnesses at Godman. The balloons were carrying equipment being used to listen into radio transmissions around the world.

Huge balloons were used to lift equipment.

Too little oxygen

Stories quickly began to circulate that Captain Mantell had in fact been killed by a "death ray" fired from the UFO. Yet a medical examination of his body proved that he had been killed by the impact of his plane hitting the ground. Flying above 6,700m (22,000ft) without an oxygen supply, Captain Mantell would have suffered from a condition called anoxia. This means his brain would have been deprived of oxygen, resulting in unconsciousness. His plane would have continued to climb, out of control, and the engine would have eventually cut out due to lack of oxygen, causing the plane to crash.

Following orders

Captain Mantell was a very experienced pilot. This fact raises the question: why did he break all the rules and fly too high without oxygen?

An intelligence officer working for the US Air Force at the Pentagon has since admitted that, during this period, Air Force pilots had been given a set of secret orders. The orders stated that if an Unidentified Flying Object was sighted, they were to capture it at any cost. These orders may help to explain Captain Mantell's relentless and suicidal pursuit of the UFO.

IDENTIFIED FLYING OBJECTS

Thousands of UFO sightings are reported every year. After investigation, UFOlogists agree that almost 95 per cent of these can be explained by natural or man-made objects. Once a UFO has been identified, it is called an IFO (an Identified Flying Object).

Mistaken identity

The most common objects mistaken for UFOs are stars, the planet Venus, the lights of aircraft, weather balloons and satellites. Up to 5 per cent of reported UFOs turn out to be the moon.

Look again

Here are just some of the things that people have mistaken for UFOs.
    The photograph below appears to show a fleet of UFOs.

In fact it shows a collection of clouds called lenticular (lens-shaped) clouds. They occasionally form when air rises above hills.
    Ball lightning is another very rare phenomenon which can confuse observers. The lightning usually appears as a sphere of glowing light, about 20cm (8in) across. The lightning crackles as it rolls slowly across the sky, and the spheres of light can last for several minutes.

Ball lightning photographed at Sankt Gallenkirch, Austria, in 1978

Bizarre explanations

Some explanations of UFOs can be very strange. A UFO reported in Lubbock, Texas in 1951, was probably a flock of geese. The city lights reflected on the underside of their white bodies.

An alien spacecraft over Lubbock, Texas?

In 1966, the crew of a spacecraft called *Gemini 11* photographed a UFO in space. Years later it was identified as a Russian satellite, *Proton-3*, which burned up 36 hours after the astronauts saw it.

Lenticular clouds often look as if they are made of metal.

Case study 17: ALIENS IN THE DESERT

Date: July 2nd, 1947
Time: 9:50pm
Place: The Foster
Ranch, near Corona,
New Mexico, USA
Witness: Multiple
witnesses

THE EVENTS

An ear-splitting explosion rang out across the desert. Just thunder, thought sheep rancher Mac Brazel, as he stood on the porch of the Foster Ranch. Yet he still felt uneasy as he watched the stormy night sky.

The next day Mac rode out to check on his flock. As he paused at the top of a hill to the wipe sweat from his forehead, he suddenly noticed below him something glittering in the sunlight. A trail of wreckage littered the valley floor. It looked like the remains of a plane.

Gossip in town

Three days later, Mac went into the town of Corona for a drink. In the bar, he heard some of the customers talking about Unidentified Flying Objects.

The crash site 120km (75 miles) northwest of Roswell, 32km (20 miles) southeast of Corona

Apparently several local people had reported seeing mysterious objects speeding across the sky. Mac began to wonder whether the strange debris he had found in the desert might be the remains of a UFO.

He decided to go straight to the local sheriff's office to report his findings.

Major Marcel investigates

Having listened to Mac's story, the sheriff decided to ring Roswell Airbase. The base immediately sent an intelligence officer named Major Jesse Marcel to go into the desert with Mac and investigate the wreckage.

What Major Marcel found was unlike anything he had ever seen before.

Kneeling on the sand, he examined pieces of the debris carefully. They appeared to be made of some kind of very light metal, like foil. Amongst the debris, there were little rods with symbols on them. When Jesse tested the debris, he found it couldn't be cut or burned. If he crumpled it up, it quickly returned to its original shape.

Another mysterious discovery

Meanwhile, 290km (180 miles) to the southeast, Grady Barnett stood rigid with terror.

The crashed saucer and its strange crew found by Grady Barnett

While working in the desert, Grady had come across a strange disk-shaped aircraft that had crashed into a hillside.

Strewn around the craft were what appeared to be the bodies of its crew. He moved closer, to get a better look. But what he saw made him freeze with horror.

A strange crew

The four bodies were abnormally thin, with big hairless heads, large eyes and small, slit-like mouths. They were only 1.4m (4ft 6in) tall. Their arms were long and their hands had only four fingers. They were definitely not human.

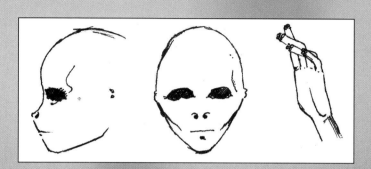

Walter Henn drew pictures of the aliens from a description given by someone who claimed to have seen their bodies.

Case study 17: ALIENS IN THE DESERT

Enter the army

Before Barnett could explore further, a US Army jeep roared up and a troop of soldiers descended on the crash site. They had been alerted by a pilot who had seen the damaged saucer from the air. One officer told Barnett to leave immediately and to tell no one about what he had seen. The soldiers sealed off the area until they had removed every trace of the debris.

That night, transporter planes flew out of Roswell Airbase under heavy guard, taking the crash wreckage to Wright-Patterson Airbase, Ohio.

Alerting the press

At noon the next day, an Information Officer at Roswell Airbase issued a statement which sent local newspapers crazy with excitement: a flying saucer had been found in the desert outside Corona.

Major Marcel posed for the press with debris from a weather balloon.

Hours later, the airbase issued a new statement. The saucer story was a mistake. The crash debris was only a weather balloon. Reporters were invited to examine the fragments.

Held in isolation

Meanwhile, soldiers were sent immediately to take Mac Brazel into custody. He was held in isolation, safely kept away from any press reporters. The only statement he was allowed to make was one that confirmed the Army's new story.

Nobody knows what threats were made to ensure Mac never talked of what he had seen in the desert. But after his release, he didn't even discuss it with the members of his own family.

On July 8th, 1947, The *Roswell Daily Record* reported the UFO story on its front page.

New investigations

For 30 years the events at Roswell were pretty much forgotten. Then, in 1978, they caught the attention of a UFOlogist named Stanton T. Friedman, who launched a detailed investigation of his own. He traced 200 people who had witnessed some aspect of the incident. Several witnesses said that they had seen the four aliens retrieved from the saucer. One even claimed to have watched autopsies performed on the bodies at Roswell Airbase.

A mysterious guest

A story began to circulate that one of the saucer's crew had survived the crash. Remaining alive for over a year, it was cared for in a top-secret facility. The alien finally died of an infection that would have been relatively harmless to humans, but against which its body had no natural resistance.

An anonymous package

In 1984, there was an exciting new development in the Roswell story. Two UFOlogists received a package through the post. Inside was a roll of 35mm film. There was no clue to who had sent it.

Once developed, the film revealed a top-secret document, dated November 18th, 1952. It appeared to have been prepared for US President Dwight D. Eisenhower.

The documents confirmed that a saucer had crashed near Roswell in 1947, and that wreckage and four alien beings had been recovered.

The documents are now known as the Majestic-12 documents, because they include a letter from Harry Truman, President of the USA in 1947, to his Secretary of Defense, instructing him to proceed with a mysterious operation called Majestic-12.

Caught on film

In 1995, sensational news broke that the British UFO Research Association had been given a film that had been shot secretly during an autopsy performed on an alien at Roswell.

The film showed a small, humanoid alien with no hair, large eyes, tiny nose and mouth. It had six digits on each hand and foot.

Many UFOlogists believe that the Roswell film is a hoax. The man who released it refuses to let the film be tested to confirm what year it was made, nor will he reveal the identity of the cameraman who filmed the autopsy.

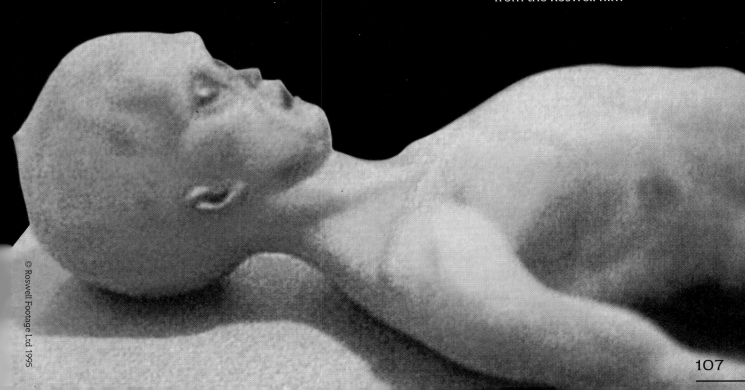

A picture of the alien taken from the Roswell film

Case study 17: THE ASSESSMENT

The Roswell Incident, as it is now known, is probably the best known UFO story. Countless claims have been made about what really happened.

Project Mogul

In 1994, the Air Force admitted that the fragments shown at the press conference in 1947 were not pieces of the debris found outside Corona. They were pieces of a Rawin Sonde weather balloon. They claimed the debris found outside Corona was from a Project Mogul balloon. Project Mogul balloons were designed to carry metal "listening" discs that were used to spy on the Soviet Union.

A Rawin Sonde balloon

Top-secret tests

It seems probable that what crashed in the desert was a top-secret device that was being tested by the government. Scientists at White Sands missile range, near Roswell, were testing thousands of pieces of military equipment at this time.

Mystery material

Investigators believe that the strange metallic material Major Marcel examined may have been an early form of polyethylene. It was indeed invented in 1947, and it would have behaved in the manner Marcel described in his tests.

Nuclear weapons

In 1947, Roswell was the home base for the world's only airborne combat unit trained to handle and drop nuclear bombs. Therefore, the transport planes seen secretly leaving the airbase under heavy guard on July 8th, were more likely to have contained nuclear weapons than an alien saucer.

Crash test dummies

On June 24th, 1997, the US Air Force revealed that during the 1940s, experiments were conducted in the area. Crash test dummies were thrown from high altitude research balloons. This might explain the "aliens" seen in the desert.

Dummies like these were used in government tests.

Hangar 84 at Roswell Air Field. Some UFOlogists believe it stores some UFO wreckage, and that an autopsy was carried out on an alien being here.

RAAF HANGAR 84

WHAT DO ALIENS LOOK LIKE?

Over the years, thousands of aliens have been encountered. UFOlogists base their ideas of what Extra Terrestrials look like on the details of these sightings. Few photographs have ever been taken of aliens. Those that exist are too indistinct to give us much information about their appearance.

The pictures on this page are all based on witnesses' descriptions of alien beings.

A huge variety

The descriptions witnesses have given of the aliens vary hugely. Red, blue, green and silver creatures have been sighted. Some beings wear robes or uniforms, others wear nothing at all. There are tall, heavily built aliens and tiny, thin ones. An Extra Terrestrial spotted in Venezuela was completely covered in hair, while another seen in Kentucky, USA, appeared to be made of metal. In 1973, an alien seen in Missisippi, USA, was described as having elephant-like skin and spikes on its head.

Many accounts of close encounters describe humanoid aliens, such as this one. Their bodies are often described as silvery, and they have large, insect-like eyes.

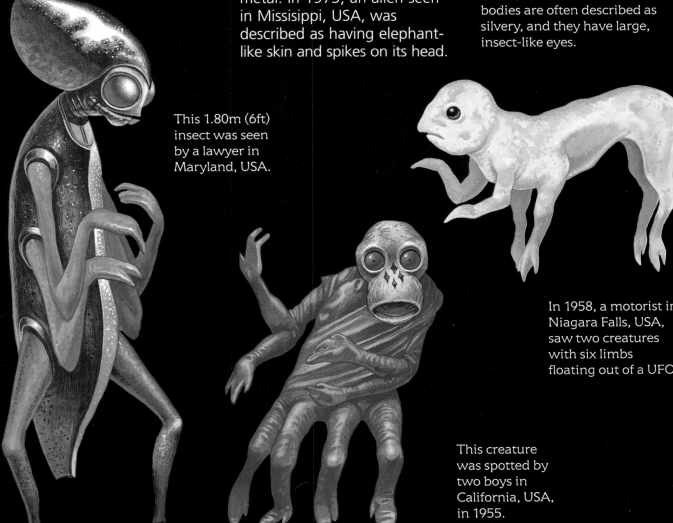

This 1.80m (6ft) insect was seen by a lawyer in Maryland, USA.

In 1958, a motorist in Niagara Falls, USA, saw two creatures with six limbs floating out of a UFO

This creature was spotted by two boys in California, USA, in 1955.

Case study 18: TWO HOURS MISSING

Date: September 19th, 1961
Time: 3:00am
Place: Lancaster, New Hampshire, USA
Witness: Betty and Barney Hill

THE EVENTS

As the alien drove the long needle deeper and deeper into her navel, Betty Hill screamed.

Sitting bolt upright in bed, she realized she was having

The Hills' car was the only one on the dark, lonely road.

another of those terrible nightmares. This time, Betty decided, she would find out what had really happened that night two years ago to cause her such terror.

Heading home

The night in question was September 19th, 1961. Betty and her husband, Barney, had been enjoying a much needed vacation in Canada. Warnings of a hurricane moving along the East Coast had prompted them to attempt to drive all through the night to get home to Portsmouth, New Hampshire.

That was how they found themselves heading south on Highway 3, which winds through the White Mountains.

It was Betty who first noticed the bright light up ahead. Barney said it was probably an aircraft, or even a satellite that had strayed off course.

At Indian Head

As the light drew nearer, Betty became convinced it was following them. Just outside the town of Lancaster, on a stretch of the road known as Indian Head, Barney slowed the car down, trying desperately to make out what was causing the bright light.

Eventually, he pulled over and switched off the engine.

Barney could see strange figures in the spaceship above him.

In a trance

Taking his binoculars from the back seat, Barney got out and walked toward the light. It was now hovering at tree level, only 15m (50ft) away.

Suddenly, Betty grew anxious. She cried out to Barney to come back. But, as if in a trance, he didn't seem to hear her. He just kept walking into the light.

The White Mountains, New Hampshire

A strange craft

Lifting the binoculars to his eyes, Barney looked at the light. It was a disk-shaped craft, and he could make out a row of windows running around its outer edge. Inside, he was sure he could see figures staring down at him through the lighted windows.

Then Barney panicked. He raced back to the car and jumped into the driver's seat. Fumbling with the ignition key, he started the engine and sped off, not stopping until they reached their home in Portsmouth, New Hampshire.

Case study 18: TWO HOURS MISSING

Missing time

Confused and alarmed, Betty reported their experience to a local UFOlogist. When he questioned them about the evening, a disturbing fact came to light. Their journey home from Lancaster had taken far longer than it should have. Two hours were missing.

Their story, however, was just one of thousands the UFOlogist had to investigate and it went to the bottom of his pile of cases.

Nightmares

Then the nightmares started. In her dreams, Betty was back in the car on Highway 3. She decided to seek help from a doctor in Boston, who used hypnosis on patients to find out the causes of their anxieties.

Under hypnosis

Dr. Simon was stunned by what he heard. Under hypnosis, Betty and Barney described in detail the events of September 19th.

Dr. Simon

Their stories were frighteningly similar. With their voices betraying their fear, they spoke of finding the road blocked by a group of strange beings. The beings were not very tall, but they had large pear-shaped heads.

On board a UFO

The next thing they knew, Betty and Barney found themselves floating up out of their car and into a spaceship.

Once inside, they were subjected to a series of medical examinations, during which samples were taken from their bodies.

Betty remembered the pain of a long needle that was inserted into her navel. Was this the pain that had tortured her in her dreams for so many nights?

A map of the stars

Throughout the examinations, the aliens kept talking to Betty and Barney. They didn't speak with their mouths, but seemed able to communicate with their thoughts.

After the tests, one of the creatures took Betty on a tour of the spaceship. The alien showed her a chart. When she asked for an explanation of the chart, the alien told her that the pattern of lines and dots was a star map. It showed the trading routes the aliens followed through space.

The alien assured Betty that she wouldn't remember any details of her experiences on the spacecraft once she had been returned to her car. However, Betty swore that she would.

Back to Earth

Somehow the couple found themselves back in their car. The UFO departed, lighting up the sky with an orange glow.

Later, when the Hill's examined their car, they found strange patches on it where the paint had been removed to reveal the metal underneath.

When Dr. Simon brought the Hills out of their trances, they were shocked to discover what they had recounted.

The road ahead of the Hills was blocked by unearthly beings.

Case study 18: THE ASSESSMENT

The Hills were a highly respectable couple, who had no reason to lie about their experiences. However, an examination of the facts of the case casts doubts on their story.

Radar report

Pease Air Force Base, whose radar covers the Indian Head area, reported tracking an unknown object in the early hours of September 19th, 1961. So there is little doubt the Betty and Barney Hill did see a UFO that night.

Missing time

The Hills claimed that they could not account for the extra two hours that their homeward journey took.

Missing time is a common experience of many people who claim to have been abducted. However, it is possible that the time the Hills spent watching the strange light in the sky, and stopping to get a closer look through binoculars, may have accounted for two hours.

Nightmares

Barney's and Betty's account of their abduction experiences were remarkably similar. However, it is probable that Betty would have described her dreams to Barney. Under hypnosis, Barney may have recounted her version of events, genuinely believing that he too had experienced them.

Star map

Under hypnosis, Betty drew the star map the alien had shown her. In 1974, Marjorie Fish, an amateur astronomer, constructed another map based on Betty's. She decided that the pattern suggested the aliens came from Zeta Reticuli, a star system about 3.7 light years away from Earth.

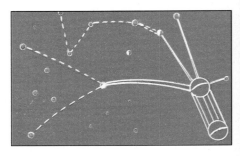

Betty's star map, with lines showing the aliens' trade routes

However, Carl Sagan, a famous astronomer, used computers to study Marjorie Fish's map, and found that the Zeta Reticuli star system bore little similarity to Betty's star map.

Carl Sagan

Many sightings

After Barney died in 1969, Betty reported many encounters with aliens. As a result, many people began to doubt the truth of her original story.

Betty and Barney Hill with Barney's picture of the alien spacecraft.

ALIEN SPACE TRAVEL

The distances that separate the planetary systems in our galaxy are vast. If aliens are visiting Earth, they have developed technological capabilities far beyond our own to make such incredible journeys possible.

A Bell X-1 plane, which was flown at supersonic speeds in 1947

Light years away

To describe distances in our galaxy astronomers use "light years". Light is the fastest thing in the Universe. It travels at 300,000km (186,000 miles) per second, and one light year is the distance light travels in a year – 9.46 million million km (5.8 million million miles).

Our galaxy is 100,000 light years across. To travel the vast distances from galaxy to galaxy or even from one planetary system to another, Extra Terrestrials would have to have developed a spacecraft that can move at the speed of light.

Unearthly speeds

Scientists believe that it is not possible to travel at the speed of light. However, they used to think that it was impossible to travel faster than the speed of sound, until a Bell X-1 plane flew at supersonic speeds in 1947.

In the future, new understanding of the physics of the Universe may enable humans to build craft that can travel at the speed of light or faster. In 1,000 years time, it may be possible to cross the Universe in minutes.

Great journeys

Other planetary systems are light years away from Earth, so even if aliens could travel at the speed of light, their journey to Earth would take many years. In human terms, this is a long journey, because humans only live for about 80 years. But different living things have different life spans. For example, bristlecone pines in California, USA, live for nearly 5,000 years. For all we know, aliens may live for thousands of years, and could, therefore, easily undertake journeys that lasted hundreds of years.

Shortcuts

Another possible theory is that aliens may have discovered shortcuts through space. Some scientists believe that there may be holes or distortions in space caused by the forces of gravity. These may create bridges, bringing two objects on different sides of the Universe closer together.

This amazing alien spaceship was made for a film called *Close Encounters of the Third Kind*.

Date: November 5th, 1975
Time: 6:15pm
Place: Apache Sitgreaves National Forest, near Heber, Arizona, USA
Witness: Travis Walton

THE EVENTS

Once all the gear was safely stowed away in the truck, Mike Rogers and his crew of six forestry workers set off through the pine forest, heading back to the town of Snowflake.

Light ahead

Just as they reached the top of a hill, Mike slammed on the truck's brakes. Up ahead, hovering above the ground, was a disk-shaped object.

From the truck, the men stared at the strange object in their way.

It was over 6m (20ft) wide and 2.5m (8ft) high, and glowing with an amber light.

The crew froze with fear, all except 22-year-old Travis Walton. He scrambled out of the truck, and walked toward the UFO.

As he drew closer, the strange craft began to vibrate ominously. Losing his nerve, Travis turned and tried to run back to the truck.

Struck by a beam

Suddenly a beam of green-blue light, like a laser beam, shot out from the base of the hovering disk. It hit Travis with such force that it sent him spinning around and threw him violently to the ground.

With a shriek of terror, Mike Rogers stepped on the accelerator pedal and the truck sped away, along the logging track. One of the crew looked back, but he had to shield his eyes. Travis's body was completely enveloped by the light.

Travis Walton was struck by a blinding ray of light from the UFO.

Deserters

As the truck bounced along the track, the crew sat in silent horror. They had left their friend out there all alone. He might be terribly injured or even dead.

Reluctantly, Mike swung the truck around and drove back. They arrived back at the crest of the hill in time to see the spacecraft rise up and speed away. Travis had disappeared.

After that, Mike didn't slow down until he reached Snowflake. He drove straight to the sheriff's office and told him the strange story.

Search party

A full-scale search was launched immediately. The police, together with a band of volunteers, scoured the forest for Travis. Too terrified to go back, three of the forestry crew refused to join the search party. The sheriff's men spread out along the track, peering through the trees and shouting Travis's name. All they heard was sound of an owl screeching.

Murder suspects

Despite an intensive search, after three days the police had found no clue to the disappearance. They turned their attentions to the forestry crew. Maybe the whole story was a hoax, or even a cover-up for murder. Had the crew killed Travis and then invented the bizarre UFO story to cover their tracks?

Questions

Sheriff Ellison had all the remaining members of the crew brought in. Pounding his fist on the table, he demanded to know where Travis's body was hidden. But the men still insisted that they didn't know anything else. They seemed genuinely upset. One man wept. Even Sheriff Ellison found it hard to believe they were just acting.

Lie detection

A lie-detector machine was brought in. These register the level of stress in a subject by measuring changes in heartbeat and sweat rate. A person telling lies usually exhibits more stress than one who is telling the truth.

One by one the men were tested, but all passed. They were telling the truth. The sheriff had to let them go.

Case study 19: KIDNAPPED BY ALIENS

A phone call

In the middle of the night, the telephone woke Travis's sister. It was Travis. Six days after his disappearence, there he was on the other end of the line. He told her that he was in a phone booth just outside town.

When Travis's brother reached the phone booth, he saw Travis, wild-eyed, bedraggled and exhausted.

Travis's story

Back home, Travis began to tell his incredible story. He recalled the bright light in the sky and the ray of light hitting him. He thought he must have been knocked unconscious by the impact of the ray, because the next thing he remembered was lying on a cold, hard table in a brightly lit room. He decided that he must be in hospital; so he called for a nurse.

Aliens on board

At that moment Travis's blood ran cold. Instead of a nurse or a doctor, three monstrous alien creatures appeared, leaning over him. He stared aghast at their hairless heads, huge eyes, and slit-like mouths.

Searching desperately for a weapon, Travis seized a piece of equipment and swung it at the aliens. Visibly alarmed, they rushed out of the room.

Three hideous creatures peered down at Travis.

This picture, taken from *Fire in the Sky* (1993), shows Travis kept in a cocoon on board an alien craft.

Bolt for freedom

Travis ran out of the room, sprinted along a corridor and into another room. Gazing around him, he saw an amazing view of the Universe, with its galaxies and stars. He realized that he was aboard a craft, shooting through space.

Man in a helmet

Travis spun around. A being had entered the room, a humanoid figure. It led him out of the UFO, into a vast building. Around him, Travis saw more saucer-shaped craft. He began to question the beings: Where was he? What was happening? But he was just told to lie down, and a mask was placed over his face. The next thing he knew, he was standing on a highway. Travis managed to drag himself to a phone and call his sister, before collapsing.

Many people believe Travis Walton's abduction was a hoax. They think he may have made up his story, but they don't know why he did it.

A broken contract

Mike Rogers' crew had a forestry contract, but they were falling behind schedule. With winter coming, they would have been unable to finish the job until spring. By inventing the bizarre abduction story the crew may have hoped to distract attention from their failure and to receive payment for the work they had already completed.

A practical joker

Travis Walton had a criminal record, and was a notorious practical joker. He may have come up with the idea of the hoax himself. Investigators discovered that he was very interested in UFOs and even owned many books on the subject.

To support his claims, however, Travis took a lie-detector test, which appears to confirm he really believed that he had been abducted by aliens.

Sticking together

Any crew member who had decided to come forward and expose the abduction as a hoax would have been richly rewarded for his story. However, all seven men have stuck to their accounts since 1975.

Hallucinations

Some people have suggested the forestry crew were hallucinating when they saw Travis Walton abducted. But it is unlikely that six men would have shared the same hallucination.

Missing for five days

In the forest, Travis Walton may have been hit by a bolt of lightning. If this had knocked him unconscious, he might have lain undiscovered for five days, despite the search. This seems unlikely, however, because he would have suffered from severe exposure.

The blow may have caused Travis to lose his memory. He could have wandered around lost, or checked into a motel to recover. This is unlikely though, because despite widespread publicity about the abduction, no one reported seeing Travis Walton during the five days that he was missing.

Travis Walton

Case study 20: UFO OVER NEW YORK

Date: November 30th, 1989
Time: 3:00am
Place: Manhattan Island, New York, USA
Witnesses: Multiple witnesses

THE EVENTS

Something terrible was about to happen. Linda could sense it. The hairs on her neck were prickling with fear, and a numbness crept gradually through her body.

It was 3:00am, and Linda Cortile was in bed. Turning to her husband who was asleep beside her, she shook him and shouted his name – but he didn't stir.

When a small creature with grey skin and intense, shiny black eyes appeared in the doorway, Linda knew what was happening. It had happened before. She was being abducted by aliens.

Totally paralyzed

With the last drop of energy in her body, Linda picked up a pillow and threw it at the approaching alien. But the pillow fell short of its target, and Linda could do nothing more to protect herself. She couldn't even lift her arms because her body was totally paralyzed. Thankfully, her mind went blank.

When she came to, Linda found herself back in her bedroom, lying in her bed.

Signs of life

Frantic with the fear that the aliens had killed her family, Linda ran into her sons' room. The two boys were lying completely still, and didn't

A ghostly creature stood in the doorway.

appear to be breathing. Linda's heart froze with terror. Seizing a small mirror, she held it under each of their noses in turn. A wave of relief flooded through her as she saw the glass mist over with their breath. They were in an unnaturally deep sleep – but at least they were still alive.

Seeking help

Linda had first gone to UFOlogist Budd Hopkins in April 1989. She wanted help. She was inexplicably certain that she had been abducted by aliens 20 years earlier.

Budd often used hypnosis to help people remember experiences of which they had no conscious memory. Under hypnosis, Linda relived an abduction experience.

Now, only seven months after her first visit to Budd, Linda was sure that she had been abducted again.

Linda Cortile

Under hypnosis

Budd put Linda into a hypnotic trance and told her to recount the events of the night of November 30th, 1989, after an alien had appeared in her bedroom. This was her amazing story.

Linda said that she floated above the rooftops in a beam of light.

Surrounded

There wasn't just one alien, there were four or five of them. Staring at her with their cold, black, shiny eyes, they terrified Linda. Silently, they approached her as she lay on the bed, powerless to move.

Then they lifted her up, holding her without actually touching her body. They took her to the window. Outside she could see a bright blue-white light. Then suddenly they all drifted through the closed window, as if it wasn't there.

Outside her apartment building, 12 floors above the ground, Linda floated in the beam of light.

Then the aliens began to levitate her, taking her up toward the belly of their spaceship. It was a saucer-shaped craft which was hovering high over the rooftops on New York.

Linda was petrified at the sight of the aliens' ghastly probes.

On board

On board the craft, Linda watched terror-stricken, as the aliens crowded around her with instruments and probes in their spindly hands. She was subjected to a terrifying medical examination.

But then the next thing she remembered, she was back in her bed.

Abduction witnesses

At first, Budd didn't think Linda's story exceptional. He had heard hundreds of similar claims. But 15 months later, he changed his mind. A letter arrived at his office. It had no return address. It appeared to be from two police officers. They only signed their first names – Richard and Dan.

They wrote of an experience that had disturbed them deeply for over a year.

On secret service

On the night of November 30th, 1989, Richard and Dan had been escorting a major political figure to New York's heliport. Everything was going perfectly smoothly, until they crossed Brooklyn Bridge. Suddenly the engine of the limousine they were using cut out. As they sat mystified in the silent car, both the police officers and their important passenger saw an incredible sight out of the car windows.

An angel

High above them, a woman in a flowing white nightgown sprang out of an open window, followed by three, small, ugly humanoid figures. Like an angel, she floated through the air and into a saucer-shaped craft. With her were four very strange-looking creatures.

Once the group had disappeared inside the UFO, it sped away over the city, toward the East River. Not far from pier 17, behind the Brooklyn Bridge, the craft glowed vivid red, and then, without slowing down, the craft plunged under the surface of the water and disappeared.

Scarcely able to believe what they had seen and worried for the woman's safety, the police officers waited beside the river. They watched the surface of the water to see if the spacecraft would reemerge and bring the woman back, but after waiting half an hour they gave up hope.

The UFO plunged into the river, just beside Brooklyn Bridge.

More evidence

In November 1991, another startling letter arrived at Budd's office. It was from a woman who Budd calls Janet Kimble – although this is not her real name. She explained that on the night of November 30th, 1989, she had been driving across Brooklyn Bridge when her car mysteriously broke down.

Looking around her, Janet realized that all the lights along the bridge were out, and the other cars on the bridge seemed to have stopped too.

As she got out of her car to see what was happening, Janet witnessed an amazing sight. A woman surrounded by several aliens floated into a UFO.

Mysteriously, Janet's story matched that of Linda and of the two police officers in many of its details.

An important story

Budd realized that Linda Cortile's case might be one of the most important of all time, because her abduction had been witnessed by at least four people.

Case study 20: THE ASSESSMENT

An alien abduction witnessed by several unconnected individuals is a rare occurrence. However, there are certain factors which make the stories of the four witnesses less convincing than they might appear at first.

No witnesses

Opposite Linda Cortile's apartment block are the offices of The New York Post. At 3:00am, when Linda claims she was abducted, journalists were working in these offices. However, none of them saw anything unusual, let alone a woman floating outside their window.

No names

It is suspicious that the police officers, Dan and Richard, never agreed to meet Budd nor to reveal their true identities. The men claimed to have been worried about the woman they saw abducted, yet they waited 15 months before contacting Budd Hopkins to report what they had seen.

Power failure

In her letter, Janet Kimble described a power failure on Brooklyn Bridge which affected other cars. However, none of the other motorists involved ever reported the incident.

Coincidence

It seems an incredible coincidence that all the people who claim to have witnessed Linda Cortile's abduction contacted Budd Hopkins rather than another UFOlogist.

Mystery man

Many UFOlogists suggest that the man the two police officers were escorting was Senõr Perez de Cuellar, who was then the Secretary General of the United Nations. Although there is no official record of a political figure using the heliport on the night of November 30th, the

Senõr Perez de Cuellar

mission was top-secret, and may not have been recorded.

Officials from the United Nations insist that Senõr de Cuellar was at home in his bed at 3:00am on the night in question. In addition, Perez de Cuellar himself has never spoken about the incident. If a figure of de Cuellar's international standing did confirm that he had witnessed Linda Cortile floating through the air, this truly would be the abduction story of the century.

The offices of the
New York Post

INDEX

INDEX

CREDITS

Every effort has been made to trace the copyright holders of the material in this book. If any rights have been omitted, the publishers offer to rectify this in any subsquent editions following notification. The publishers are grateful to the following organizations and individuals for their permission to reproduce material: (t=top, b=bottom, r=right, l=left)

p7 Bodleian Library: Von Bruder Rauschen, 1835, title page woodcut; p8-9 Graham Morris; p9 (bl) Graham Morris; (br) Graham Morris; p10-11 Comstock 1998; p11 (tr) (both) Mirror Syndication International; p12 (tr) Maurice Grosse; (bl) photographed with thanks to Olympus Cameras; p13 (b) Mirror Syndication International; p14 (tr) Fortean Picture Library; p18 (bl) Fortean Picture Library; p19 (tr) Fortean Picture Library; p20 *Ecce Homo* by Vicente Juan Macip (Juan de Juanes) (c. 1510-79), Prado, Madrid/Bridgeman Art Library, London/New York; p21 (br) Fortean Picture Library; p22 (br) Images Colour Library; p23 (t) Bodleian Library: Mal. 210. Dr. Faustus, 1631, title page woodcut; (b) K F Lord/Fortean Picture Library; p25 Popperfoto; p29 Mary Evans Picture Library; p30 (l) Guy Lyon Playfair/Fortean Picture Library; p31 (tr) Dimitri Ilic, Comstock 1998; p32 Comstock 1998; p33 (r) Nigel Smith/Hutchison; p34 (r) Copyright 1976/1993 Larry E Arnold/Fortean Picture Library; p35 (bl) Tony Stone Images; (b) Tony Stone Images; (r) Tony Stone Images; p38 (both) Topham Picturepoint; p39 (tr) Topham Picturepoint;

p41 (footprints) W. Perry Conway/Corbis; p43 (tl) Topham Picturepoint; (tr) English Heritage Photo Library; (b) English Heritage Photo Library; p44 (br) Camera Press; p45 (tr) Topham Picturepoint; (b) TRH Pictures; p46 (r) Topham Picturepoint; p47 (both) Jeff Roberts, News International Syndication; p48 (l) Mary Evans Picture Library; (tr) Mary Evans Picture Library, Society for Psychical Research; p49 (tl) Topham Picturepoint; p50-51 (mountains) Topham Picturepoint; p51 (br) Associated Press; p53 (both) Associated Press; p55 (br) Camera Press; p56 (tl) Warner Bros. (courtesy of The Ronald Grant Archive); (tr) Topham Picturepoint; (b) Pictorial Press; p57 (tl) Corbis-Bettman/UPI; (tr) Fortean Picture Library; (r) AKG London/AP; (b) Corbis (UK); p58 (l) Rex Features, Julian Makey; (tr) Mary Evans Picture Library; (br) Hulton Getty; p60-61 (t) TRH Pictures; p62 (r) Sylvia Pitcher/The Weston Collection; p63 (l) Associated Press; (on screen) AKG/AP; p65 (tr) Guy Lion Playfair/Fortean Picture Library; p66 Derek Stafford/Fortean Picture Library; p67 Mary Evans Picture Library; p68 (tr) Andreas Trottman/Fortean Picture Library; p69 (bl) ©The British Museum

CREDITS (continued)

p69 (br) Andreas Trottman/Fortean Picture Library; p70 ©Patrick Ottaway; p73 (tl) Adam Hart-Davis/Fortean Picture Library (b) Photostage/ Donald Cooper; p74 Photograph by Mark Gunn; p75 Photograph by Mark Gunn; p76 (bl) Detail by permission of the British Library 1007628.011 - the image has been digitally manipulated (br) The Ancient Art and Architecture Collection Ltd; p77 (tl) Detail by courtesy of the National Portrait Gallery (tr) Janet & Colin Bord/Fortean Picture Library (br) *Cromwell after the Battle of Marston Moor* (oil on canvas) by Ernest Crofts (1847-1911) Towneley Hall Art Gallery and Museum, Burnley, Lancashire/ Bridgeman Art Gallery, London/New York; p78 (tr) By permission of the British Library 1007628.011 (b) Clive Barda/Performing Arts Library; p79 (r) Fortean Picture Library; p80 Wallcovering reproduced by kind permission of Crown Wallcoverings, a division of The Imperial Home Decor Group (UK) Limited, Darwen, England; p83 (both) Science Photo Library; p84 (bl) Fortean Picture Library (br) Marina Jackson/Fortean Picture Library; p85 (tr) Tony O'Rahilly/Fortean Picture Library (bl) Mary Evans/Peter Underwood (br) National Maritime Museum, Greenwich, London; p86 Dr Elmar R. Gruber/Fortean Picture Library; p87 (both) Dr Elmar R. Gruber/Fortean Picture Library; p88 (bl) With permission from Andrew MacKenzie (tr) With permission from José Martínez Romero; p89 Mary Evans/John Cutten; p90 (bl) Lockheed Martin/TRH Pictures (b) UPI/Corbis (tr) TRH Pictures; p91 (bl) UPI/Corbis (br) Popperfoto; p93 UPI/Corbis; p94 UPI/Corbis; p95 (t) Fortean Picture Library (bl) Paramount TV/The Ronald Grant Archive; p98 Science and Society Picture Library/National Museum of Photography, Film and Television; p99 Fortean Picture Library; p102 Corbis-Bettmann; p103 main image Fortean Picture Library; ball lightning, Werner Burger/Fortean Picture Library; p105 Walter Henn; p106 (bl) Fortean Picture Library; (tr) Fortean Picture Library; p107 © Roswell Footage Ltd 1995; p108 (l) US Air Force photo; (b) Dennis Stacy/Fortean Picture Library; p109 (tr) Vestron UK Ltd, courtesy of the Ronald Grant Archive; pp110-111 background, Corbis/W. Wayne Lockwood, MD; car, TRH pictures; p112 (bl) Mary Evans Picture Library; p114 (bl) Fortean Picture Library; (br) Corbis/Bettmann; p115 (bl) Columbia Pictures/The Ronald Grant Archive; (tr) TRH Pictures; pp116-117 main picture, UIP/Moviestore Collection; p116 (bl) UIP, courtesy of the Ronald Grant Archive; p119 (t) UIP/Moviestore Collection; (br) Dennis Stacy/Fortean Picture Library; p120 Dennis Stacy/Fortean Picture Library; p121 main picture, Peregrine Mendoza/Fortean Picture Library; p124 (bl) The New York Post; (r) Corbis-Bettmann/Reuters.

The material in this book has also appeared in four separate titles:
Poltergeists?, **ESP?**, **Ghosts?** and **Alien Abduction?**

Additional design work by Andrew Dixon, Russell Punter and Michael Wheatley
Additional DTP work by Zoë Wray and Michèle Busby
Additional picture research by Rebecca Gilpin

Thanks to: British UFO Research Association; Stanton T. Friedman; Andrew MacKenzie for information relating to case studies 13 and 14 in Chapter Three (Ghosts?); models Stefan Barnett, Michèle Busby, Laura Creyke, Neil Francis, Mark Howlett, Asha Kalbag, Jonathan Miller, Susannah Owen, Joe Pedley, John Russell, Katherine Starke, Chris Te-Whata, Zoë Wray and Stephen Wright